T0147010

How precious to me are your thoughts, God!
    How vast is the sum of them!
Were I to count them,
    they would outnumber the grains of sand—
    when I awake, I am still with you.

                            —Psalm 139:17–18 NIV

My Thoughts Become Your Thoughts

Hearing the Voice of God

Inspired Revelation
through a Conscious Awareness of Life's Presence

Tracy Menchenton

BALBOA.
PRESS
A DIVISION OF HAY HOUSE

Balboa Press books may be ordered through booksellers or by contacting:

Balboa Press
A Division of Hay House
1663 Liberty Drive
Bloomington, IN 47403
www.balboapress.com
1 (877) 407-4847

Because of the dynamic nature of the Internet, any web addresses or links contained in this book may have changed since publication and may no longer be valid. The views expressed in this work are solely those of the author and do not necessarily reflect the views of the publisher, and the publisher hereby disclaims any responsibility for them.

The author of this book does not dispense medical advice or prescribe the use of any technique as a form of treatment for physical, emotional, or medical problems without the advice of a physician, either directly or indirectly. The intent of the author is only to offer information of a general nature to help you in your quest for emotional and spiritual well-being. In the event you use any of the information in this book for yourself, which is your constitutional right, the author and the publisher assume no responsibility for your actions.

Any people depicted in stock imagery provided by Getty Images are models, and such images are being used for illustrative purposes only. Certain stock imagery © Getty Images.

Print information available on the last page.

ISBN: 978-1-9822-1353-4 (sc)
ISBN: 978-1-9822-1352-7 (hc)
ISBN: 978-1-9822-1354-1 (e)

Library of Congress Control Number: 2018911739

Balboa Press rev. date: 10/23/2018

Contents

Chapter 3: Inheriting the Kingdom—The Practice of Entering a Present State of Mind

Chapter 4: Your Mind's Alignment with the Reality of Life's Presence – You Are Now One with the Creator of All Existence

Chapter 5: *The Book of Life*—Remaining in the Eternal Presence of Life's Existence

Appendices

Dedication

I have dedicated this book to the three women whom I have shared my life with and deeply love.

For my dear grandmother, Beatrice, a selfless, sacrificing woman who eagerly gave of herself to others in pure love and gentle kindness: As I now have come to understand, she was a manifestation of the Christ, fully surrendered to her true identity. I had often thought, *Who are you but a reflection of God? Surely, you must be!* Oh, how easy it was and is to love you, Nanny! My love for you is eternal, as I have seen the light of Him within you. I love the Christ in you!

My beloved mother, Doris: I treasure your sacrificial heart, the selfless love that can only come from a mother, the love and care you so readily gave to each one of us. I knew your struggles and pain, and at last, the Lord gave you no more than you could bear. He called you home to His Eternal Oneness. Thank you for your love and your profound humor.

For my sweet Aliyana, my gift of love and joy: What a treasure you are to me, my very reason to live this life in its fullness. May you continually seek the Lord's Presence in every moment, experiencing His aliveness, the very peace and joy of being One with Him. May you sacrifice your self in all that you do, so that the Glory of God may be revealed in all His magnificence through you!

I dedicate my heart's wisdom to all who have suffered mentally in fear and doubt, crippled in darkness, stumbling through the unconscious mind, the very unawareness of life itself. There is a great light of awareness to be witnessed, a saving from mental anguish! Come, enter into this glorious Present state of mind, and become all you were created to be!

Acknowledgments

I can only acknowledge my awareness of the Presence of God within me. It is the Conscious Infinite Intelligence within that desires to express His words through this manuscript. I am but a scribe to His free-flowing wisdom and inspiration.

Christ in me is my awareness to the abiding Presence of Consciousness. This is the revelation of God and mystery made known.

May you become awakened to the Conscious Presence of life within and its continual *calling* you inward, to reveal your true identity. *Be transformed by the renewing of your mind* ….

Introduction

Prelude

I decided to begin this book by sharing with you some of my personal Spiritual awakening experiences. I hope to give you insight into my mind's awakening to Consciousness; my awareness of God's Presence within me. These are only some of my preliminary awakening experiences, and it would be impossible to write them all within the context of an introduction. I will attempt to give you clarity of understanding through my personal firsthand account.

I had an earnest pursuit to know God, why I was here in this moment of time, and why I felt such uncertainty or loss of control in my life. I wondered why the world, in itself, is unjust. It just did not make sense to me. Why would a Creator, an all-loving God, purposely allow the world to exist in the state it is in? Why is there so much pain, depression, darkness, and death? Why am I here? What role am I to play in this? These recurring questions came to mind from time to time, but they were certainly not the reason why I found myself questioning God or shaking my fist at Him, this go-around.

A Mind Imprisoned by Thought

Before I had received any understanding through my mind's *renewal*, this new way of *Being fully Present with life;* there was no Conscious awareness or understanding to the thoughts that would lead me astray from experiencing life's Presence, in the now. My experiences of life were essentially led by my attachment to the mind's processing of thoughts. I saw my identity as the *thinker* within my mind: the, *I, me, myself* voice within. I was the thinking, rationalizing, and seeking mind. Whatever thoughts arose within my mind, the continual chatter and internal dialogue, I followed them.

My thoughts held me captive to experience emotions and oftentimes thoughts of fear that led me down paths of worry and uncertainty. There was no purposeful direction, one might say, in the thoughts that ran rampant through my mind. It was like being taken on a roller coaster ride with no control of the ride itself. Prior to a Conscious mind of awareness, I thought my identity, this ego persona, was reality. Because I was thinking these thoughts, surely it was I who was doing the thinking; the voice of I, me, and myself were all that existed within. I was not aware that my *unconscious* mind's thinking and rationalizing had imprisoned my mind and that I was held captive by my attachment to it.

In my experience, the more my thoughts focused specifically on the ego, the more I went down paths of mental anguish. Fear, doubt, and anxiety began to creep in. The more I thought about any perceived issue without resolution, the more momentum the thoughts took within my mind. The more focus I placed on those thoughts, the more they began to expand. It was during times of great trials in my life that the incessant focusing on the problem at hand created darkness within, leaving me with very little mental peace. At times, a war raged in my mind, and I had no awareness that I held the key to end my torment instantly. I was not Consciously aware of my *Being* in those moments of life, as I gave no insight to the Present moment of life's only existence. I was not aware that I could rise above my thoughts in surrender of them and experience a stillness of *just Being Present* in the observation and acceptance of life's reality. Rising above my thoughts would lead me to a refuge within my mind, a peaceful and content *Present* state of mind.

Enlightenment: Awakening to the Awareness of God's Presence Within

In Brokenness, a Brief Moment of Awareness

I remember one instance in particular in which darkness had enslaved my mind. The fear of the unknown, the uncertainty of my future, and all that I perceived to have recently lost weighed heavily on me for days. I had little hope and was despaired of my current situation. I had recently become a single mother to an infant child; my daughter who slept peacefully in the back of my SUV was unaware of all the changes that were taking place in her little life. I found myself driving around aimlessly with no purposeful direction, and my mind was doing the very same thing. Street after street, my mind was caught up in darkness. I was not in a state of Presence—*Being Present of mind in the now*—but was instead reflecting on the past or thinking of the future. As I reflected on the past, I was momentarily held captive by my emotions. Hurt, resentment, regret, and condemnation began to creep in. As I focused my mind on the future, I had uncertainty, doubts, worries, and anxiety. There was little belief in a positive outcome because my mind dwelled on the past pain or the uncertainty of my future. In those moments, my mind sank in a pit of despair.

In between my mind's continual chatter and run-on dialogue, I was seeking direction and guidance. I was searching for a light to shine through the darkness that had imprisoned my mind. And then next, through a brief moment of clarity, an inspiring thought: maybe I should search the radio channels for a song that would uplift me, give me some reprieve from the mental torment my thoughts were creating. As I began to search and listen to the radio channels, I heard a man speak whom I would later come to know as Dr. Stanley, a TV and radio evangelist with In Touch Ministries. As my mind was now fully Present and aware, listening rather than rationalizing and thinking, the words that were spoken in that moment seemed to have been directly voiced at me. The words had awakened my mind to the shocking revelation of what was occurring. It was as if God was talking through Dr. Stanley to commune with me. Each word spoken directly related to my heart, my brokenness, my despair, and my current situation. I was so in awe of what I was hearing that I frantically pulled over, longing to stay connected to the voice that knew me so well.

Then as quickly as I experienced the moment of clarity

through my awareness, thoughts of disbelief entered my rational mind: *How can this man know what I am feeling? How does he know my personal situation? How does he know all these things? How can he be speaking to me in this moment?* The thinking and rationalizing mind had crept in again and led me away from a moment of Being Present through a Conscious awareness with life itself. But even through my mind's rationalization, I could not dismiss what I had just experienced, its very realness; something was calling me *out of this world* to awaken to another existence. That was the first seed of a burning desire planted within me, a luring or pulling of some sort to know God more—or at the very least, to experience more of this metaphysical occurrence. *The only answer to the darkness is to seek God*, I thought. It would take many more of these awakenings before I had any understanding of my mind's transformation.

A Moment of Acceptance to Life's Presence; the Surrender of My False Self-Awareness

Several months later, I found myself back in the same city I had left a year before. I had no job and was living in a high-rental home with a small infant to care for. Indeed, I was back in the familiarity of the life I had left, the same surroundings and friends, but the darkness still followed me. I tried to ground myself with a job search, seeking childcare and even social assistance to help me provide for my daughter. I had lost everything, including my savings and my pride. I was in complete despair when every job position I applied for, even the ones for which I was overqualified, closed their doors on me. I thought my life struggle could not get any worse at that point. And then I received the call that my grandmother, who was living across the country from me, was hospitalized. I was advised that I should go back to my hometown to see her because she did not have long to live.

When I was growing up, my grandmother was the foundation that kept our family together. Through trials and difficulties, her faith in God saw us through. Her heart of unconditional love and kindness drew us all in. She was a completely self-less woman who was easy to love. Although I did not have the fullness of understanding then, she was the closest I had ever experienced to Christ's manifestation. She was always in complete surrender to God's Spirit, and I had little understanding that each time I looked into her eyes, it was God who was looking back out at me. God was with me through the vessel of my grandmother throughout my whole life. And the one person who had showed me continual sacrificial love, guidance, and support was leaving this world. This was the moment I had hoped would never come.

After returning home from my grandmother's passing, I found myself completely alone and again having to face my uncertain future. I had lost my worldly foundation, my career and relationships, and now my faithful Spiritual encourager. I had been crushed this time, and there was no way of getting up and going forward. I had no hope, and I immediately dropped to my knees in complete surrender to the war that was raging in and all around me. *In that moment, I surrendered and gave up resisting to what was*. I had come to the end of my mind's false self-awareness and surrendered to God's Presence within. *My God,* I thought, *where are You? Why have You allowed this to happen to me? I cannot go on anymore. Please God, help me get through this!* It was evident to *my self* that I was failing miserably, and struggling even in the best of moments.

During that time, my only constant desire was my desperation to know where my grandmother *knew* where she was going: home to be with God. My grandmother rarely spoke about Jesus, but she emanated His very Presence. So I began to seek Him earnestly with all I had within me. I knelt at the foot of my bed, a complete emotional mess, and I called out to the Lord, reciting the well-known Sinner's Prayer: *Forgive my sins, and come into my life, Lord*. I needed direction, guidance, mental peace, and healing. I had no idea what any of that meant—who He was or how my life would change. I just knew I could no longer go on in this world as *I perceived it to be*.

Yet what had just taken place was the most incredible freedom within my mind that I had ever experienced. I had let go of every thought that plagued me! And in *my moment of surrender or acceptance of what was*, I felt mentally free, no longer creating a mental resistance to what was occurring. Although it was momentary, I was set free from the attachment of my mind's anguish as if I had risen above it somehow. I was sitting in complete stillness of mind, with an awareness of letting go and rising above. And for a brief moment, I sat in the nothingness of my mind and became immediately aware of the emerging peace within. This incredible moment of my mind's awakening to a *Conscious awareness of Being Present* did not last long. I had no understanding of what had taken place, nor did I fully understand that I could also remain in that state of mind. I immediately plunged back into the rational mind, the mind of unawareness to life's Present moment existence.

The Calling of God: The Night and Morning Awakenings to the Voice Within

In the days following my momentary surrender to *God's Presence*, I was still suffering in periods of mental anguish, as if I was in the pit of some sort of hell. I remained mentally focused on my perceived losses and current life situation. I was trying to rationalize many things and come to some sort of resolution to my issues at hand. I had no clarity, only confusion. My mind drifted from the past and then forward to the future. I failed to *fully* rest my mind in the Present, but only to receive glimpses of these awakenings to life's reality of existence.

I prayed earnestly that I would be delivered from my mind's continual *"figuring things out,"* its place of unrest and internal conflict. I had yet to fully awaken to the understanding that letting go is a continual surrender, a *continual acceptance to the Present moment state of mind*. I was desperate to experience more of this emerging awareness to the *Presence of life* within, to experience more of *God*.

John 3:16

It was early in the morning hours, and I was in a deep sleep, when I slowly became Conscious to thoughts arising within my awareness. At first, these thoughts were soft and slowly *spoken*. Then they gradually became louder and faster, *"John 3:16, John 3:16, John 3:16!"*

What the hell, I thought. *Go to sleep Tracy; I'm exhausted.*

And the more I fought these thoughts, the louder and faster they spoke or *arose within my awareness* to them, *"John 3:16, John 3:16, John 3:16!"*

Oh my God, this is driving me insane! My brain would not shut off. I sat up in my bed, and my next thought was that *this sounds like Bible scripture*. The only Bible I had was tucked away on the top shelf of my closet, a gift from my grandmother years prior.

Again, the repetitive thoughts were pounding in my head, *"John 3:16, John 3:16, John 3:16!"*

Okay! I yelled back to the *emerging Presence within* that refused to give up.

As I reached for the Bible and began to thumb through its pages, my eyes fell upon the book of John, chapter 3, verse 16: "For God so loved the world that he gave his one and only Son, that whoever believes in him shall not perish but have eternal life." *Hmm*, I thought, *what a strange coincidence*, and I fell back to sleep. This awakening during the middle of the night was certainly not my last encounter with the internal voice. And in the days and months to follow, quite often I was awakened at night or early in the morning with the awareness of a flow of profound wisdom emerging within my mind—a free-flowing interchange of insight and my understanding of it.

Groggy and half asleep, I would fumble in the dark for my pen and paper to write down the thoughts. Like a tap that had been turned on, wisdom flowed seamlessly and then ended abruptly. The Lord would wake me night after night, encouraging me to write all that He had given me. Oh how I loved His awakenings, the revelation of *His Being* within me! How incredible it was, and is, to hear the Living God speak to me, piercing my Conscious awareness, and giving me exactly what I need in that moment.

Question God, and Wisdom Answers

During the early days and months of my solitude and prayer time with God, I would be the speaker and question Him on things about my personal life, the world's issues, and who He really was. There was a lot I wanted to know, and I would fall asleep with these puzzling questions on my mind. I was always talking to Him but had little understanding at this point that I could actually *hear* from Him.

I recalled my first encounter with Dr. Stanley's radio podcast and thought, *Why not continue to listen to the show for some of my answers?* I began to experience what I first perceived as little coincidences. I soon began to realize that my questions to God about different things became the topics of discussion on Dr. Stanley's radio podcasts the next morning. The topic was always the very question I had raised in prayer the night before. Many times, this exact occurrence happened, and each time I would think, *This is such a coincidence*, until one morning I realized it was no coincidence at all. Again, God was speaking to me through Dr. Stanley.

My rational mind could not comprehend what was taking place. To my amazement, I began to enjoy these strange occurrences, asking in prayer and waiting eagerly for the morning show to come on the radio. *You have got to be kidding me!* Time after time, God continued to answer my questions and inquisitive prayers.

My Awareness of a Collective Conscious Presence Within

The Bicycle

It was the spring of 2013, and my daughter was turning two years old. My heart was heavy at that time because I had no money to buy her anything of material significance. As I looked over the Toys "R" Us flyer, I noticed a beautiful pink bike. This bike was the kind of bike for toddlers where the parent could assist its motion with a long handle that stretched upward. *This would be perfect for her!* I thought. But with deep despair, I knew it was out of my hands to provide.

So I prayed, asking God to provide some way for me to buy my daughter this birthday gift. I thanked Him and thought of it no more, until one week later when I received a phone call from my discipleship mentor from our local church. Barb had been a dear friend to me during those earlier times, teaching me about God's ways and showing me God's love through her countless gifts of sacrifice. When I picked up the phone, I was immediately faced with Barb's frustration. She said that she had been certain about a gift she wanted to buy for my daughter, but she was worried because she felt she was never good at choosing gifts for people. She felt compelled to call me and ask me what I thought about her gift idea. She went on to say that there was a little bike she had seen that *really spoke to her*, and that Aliyana *should have* this bike for her birthday. Perplexed at her conviction, I went on to say that strangely enough, I had my heart set on a bike for her. Barb continued and said that she was thinking of this *little pink bike* that had a handle to assist the parent with the bike's motion.

My jaw dropped, and I had no words to say. Tears of joy streamed down my face in my silence. *I am just looking at this Toys "R" Us flyer, and I think this little pink bike would be perfect for Aliyana, what do you think?* I could only cry out loud in joy and amazement. I could not believe what was happening. My heart leaped, and not for the material bicycle but because God had heard my prayer; He knew my heart's desire. I had put my trust in Him, and He provided in a beautiful and mysterious way.

An Inspired Vision of Conscious Clarity

On another day, I had lost my cell phone. It was not only my connection with the outside world, but it held my faithful morning podcasts, my wisdom from God. After a full evening and late night search for my phone, I fell exhausted upon my bed. I thought,

God, where is it? Show me, as I am at a loss! My mind fell silent as I lay there in complete stillness almost to the point of a surrendered sleep.

Then a vision, a clear picture of my phone, flashed into my mind. It was like a detailed photograph, and it showed my phone lying facedown in the snow right next to the mailbox! I had gone out earlier that morning and checked the community mailbox down the street. I quickly jumped up, certain that I would find it there. To my amazement, not only was the phone near the mailbox, but it was facedown in the snow pile exactly as the vision conveyed. *Incredible!* I thought.

The Unexplainable Longing and Deep Desire Within Calling Me to a Place of Solitude

As my desire deepened for the Lord, *the incredible awakening to a Presence within*, I often felt an overwhelming pull to retreat to the solitude of my bedroom. It was the least distracting room of my home, and I enjoyed the quiet in there; as if I were metaphorically shutting out the whole world the minute I closed its door. As my daughter slept in her crib, I would find myself taking that time to seek a restful stillness, lying prone on my bedroom floor. With the Bible in front of me, I was eager to learn more about God's Presence and what I was experiencing within my mind. I wanted to speak to Him, but there was an unexplainable longing for a deeper connection, a desire that was emerging within me that I somehow had no control over. It was an inner pulling and calling of some sort to be in solitude, as if I was being led upstairs to my room to seek more of this *inner Presence*. I would oftentimes feel as if my mind were being led as I would fumble through the Bible scriptures. I began to seek God's wisdom, to *listen* rather than to talk and ask questions. *Does He speak?* I thought. I felt compelled to lie there with a pen and notebook, and I prayed a simple prayer to the Lord to control my mind and my thinking, to bring me peace and to heal my heart. So I lay there, silently waiting in the stillness of my mind, waiting patiently as if to hear something ....

After some time, thoughts began to emerge within my mind, and I would journal each word or series of words that arose. I began to witness the words forming sentences upon my paper. Even though I had no idea what the sentences were forming, I continued to lose *my self* in the writing, allowing every thought to be written. I began to let go and lose control of any perceived idea of what my hand would write. I was amazed that the thoughts formed perfect sentences on the paper, and the sentences flowed with ease. And then I realized I was not the One forming the thoughts into words that were in perfect sentence structure and gave perfect clarity to understanding.

Freedom from the Attachment of My Mind—Enlightened to the Conscious Presence Within

Early in my journal writings, I began to question who or what was giving me these thoughts to write. *Am I not my own thoughts? It is clear that I am not writing these words from my own understanding. If these are not my thoughts, then I must be the observer or witness to them, arising within. Who am I?*

I continued to write, forming paragraphs of profound wisdom that gave me incredible insight and understanding. And then as quickly as the thoughts arose, there was stillness within my mind again. So I sat eagerly, as if *to hear* another word. This time, a Bible verse emerged, which was quite odd as I had no understanding of the Bible, its books, or any of the scripture verses. Like an investigator with a new lead on an old case file, I thought, *Why not? I will search for this in the Bible.* After much thumbing through the pages, I stumbled upon the given scripture. To my amazement, what I read provided the same understanding I was given in my journal writing.

It was evident that I was not writing these thoughts and words, but that they were being given to me, and all this understanding was coming from the *Inner Conscious Presence within*: *God*. This soon became an exciting game of writing words of great wisdom and profound knowledge, gaining understanding in the moment of what I was writing, and then reading the given follow-up scripture that revealed the same truth about what I wrote. I was hooked! *How exciting and amazing,* I thought. I had no idea that God was *so alive* in this moment of my awareness to His Presence, speaking truth to me with inspired thoughts!

During this time, however, my rational mind was trying to comprehend what was happening and why I had all these experiences. I was delighted to be in His Presence, and this was fun, exciting, and mysterious. Like an inquisitive child, I would spend hours in solitude with Him, and we would play this game of journal writing and then Scripture revelation. I felt peace in my mind; my thoughts were grounded to the Present moment, to this *Inner Presence of just Being, One with life.* I felt refreshed and encouraged with each session of solitude. I did not fear future unknowns or thoughts of the past because my mind was deeply planted in the Present moment. I had complete trust of what was through my mind's surrender. There was no darkness to be found within my mind but *the light of Conscious awareness* to life's existence, the Present moment. My mind was fully aligned with the *now* of life, and I felt peace within. I was transcending my rationalizing and thinking mind to the listening and observing or witnessing mind, to *God's Presence.* I was fully alive, awake, and aware of His existence within me.

His Revelation: "My Thoughts Become Your Thoughts," the Inspired Emerging Words Within

I believe in You because You have revealed Yourself to me. I believe in You because I know You. I believe in You because You speak to me and awaken me to Your very Presence within. You are fully alive in me, O Lord!

I remember the experience just as if it was yesterday—how vivid and real, how awakened and truly alive I felt. God had revealed Himself to me, just as I desired and asked of Him.

It was a Sunday afternoon, and I had just put my infant daughter down in her crib for a nap. I turned on the television to the Christian Broadcasting Network, and decided I, too, would take a quick rest on the sofa. The volume on the television was very low, so as not to wake my daughter. The TV program series was one that I have watched many times before where the commentator asks his guests about their personal experiences with Jesus Christ. As I began to drift into sleep, I heard a voice coming from the television, as if the volume on it had risen. *"If you ask God to reveal Himself, He will!"* And just like that, the seed was planted! Surprisingly, I was now fully awake and aware of what I'd just heard.

Despite my earlier exhaustion, I felt an overwhelming desire to retreat to my bedroom to continue with my prayer journaling. I had been writing for months now, and the continual desire and lure was drawing me in, the overwhelming longing to be Present with Him. Like many times before, with all the thoughts that emerged within, I began to write. I had begun to doubt my journaling through my rationalizing mind, and I struggled with my identity in the writing. *Was it me? Was I the thinker, or was I the listening observer witnessing God speak to me?* And so I began like many times before: *Father, please control my thoughts, my mind, so that I only hear Your voice, and not my own, in Jesus's name.* This time would be different, however. I immediately felt a profound sense of purpose, and as I placed my journal and Bible in front of me, I asked, *Father, please reveal Yourself to me,* for I was quickly reminded of what the TV guest suggested.

I began to write a constant flow of thoughts, word after word, having no conception of what the sentences were forming. And just as had happened many times before, each sentence formed incredible wisdom and understanding on the page. *Wow!* I was on a roll this time, and my hand could not keep up with the free-flowing thoughts. I felt my wrist getting sore from the effort of writing each emerging thought so quickly. Like a fountain that was turned on in my mind, wisdom and understanding began to pour in. And then it stopped as quickly as it had started. I was in awe again of these words on my paper and the clarity and understanding I gained from receiving them. They were written with such authority, truth, and conviction.

As I sat within the stillness of my listening mind, I became aware to the emerging voice within, *"My Thoughts Become Your Thoughts,"* and then a scripture reference to my previous journal. As I began to read the given scripture, the words of that verse seemed to physically reach up from the page, and the remaining words faded into the background in an indiscernible haze. Not only what I read in that moment were the very same words I was given in my journal entry, but I could not believe how alive the words became on the page; they seemed to have jumped out from their positioning. I slammed the Bible shut, throwing it across the floor of my bedroom! *I was immediately convicted of the undeniable truth of His Presence within me.* Feelings of amazement soon became feelings of remorse: *How could I ever doubt the Lord and all that He has been teaching me these past months?* I was entering the Presence of God through my mind's Conscious awareness, sitting at His footstool, and bathing in His love and guidance for me. *How could I have ever doubted Him?*

I was captivated from that moment! Completely and fully *Consciously aware* in that Present moment that I was not alone in my mind and thoughts. It would take me a couple of years to fully understand what was taking place within my mind, this *renewing of the mind,* as the Bible teaches. I had found this incredible new freedom of surrendering the false self-awareness I was attached to, the false identity, the "I" of who *I thought* I was.

Caught Up in Awareness to Life's Revealing Purpose

I soon began to realize that the more I surrendered any thoughts of the ego, *the awareness of a false-self-identity,* the more I felt God's emerging Conscious Presence within. There was contentment with the *just Being* and *knowing,* even through the most mundane of tasks. And in the awareness of just Being One with life in the Present moment, *God,* the Conscious Presence within, would permeate me as His vessel. I was completely caught up with the Lord through my Conscious awareness of His Presence. Hours became days, and days became nights. There was very little concept of time, as it all seemed to flow into one. My awareness was fully in *Being Present of mind*, and He remained fully alive in me. Wisdom and understanding continued to flow. Direction and guidance for His purpose and plan began to unfold. God was revealing His purpose, what He desired to do through me, and this was my *calling* or *luring* inward from His Presence within.

The Call to Leave It All Behind

I felt life's direction and purpose quite early in my intimate conversations with God. I would be guided to write the words that He spoke and to share them. At that time, I had no understanding that the words I wrote would later form this manuscript. He would often bring me to Jeremiah 30:1–2: "The word that came to Jeremiah from the Lord: 'Thus says the Lord, the God of Israel: Write in a book all the words that I have spoken to you.'"

To practice the awakening of Being fully Present of mind and aware of your Consciousness within will require a sacrifice of your time spent in the world. The emerging Presence is experienced inwardly, an arising awareness when you have surrendered the mind's attachment. As the world oftentimes leads us astray with *outward* attractions and busyness, it can be very difficult or seemingly impossible to catch glimpses or to fully experience the *inner* awareness of God's Presence. The ego or the false-self awareness chooses to seek the world, that is, everything that is physically outside of us. The experience of God's Presence is only found within our *Inner Being of Consciousness*.

At times, I have drifted away from life's Presence because of my false-self awareness that leads my mind away from life's now occurring; the Present moment state of mind. The ego mind state is always discontented with what is in this moment, and it will lure us away from Being Present with life's reality in the now. We have the power to choose one state of mind over the other. I am reminded of Matthew 6:24, "No one can serve two masters. Either you will hate the one and love the other, or you will be devoted to the one and despise the other. You cannot serve both God and money." We have the power to remain in the fullness of a Present mind to allow life's purpose and destiny to be fulfilled through us.

His leading has been one of precise clarity and direction for this book. I would oftentimes wake up to His voice, His thoughts piercing my Consciousness. As if my mind were a black chalkboard, white words began to flow upon its surface. Each heading that appeared indicated the wisdom and understanding that followed. The organization of the writing became quite evident when I had the table of contents outlined on a draft piece of paper. Therefore, I am only the scribe of these inspired words, which come from my awareness to the manifestation of God within me: "knowing this first of all that no prophecy of Scripture comes from someone's own interpretation. For no prophecy was ever produced by the will of man, but men spoke from God as they were carried along by the Holy Spirit" (2 Peter 1:20–21).

This Book —Life's Intended Purpose

The purpose of this book is to share with you the truth of *the Kingdom of God*, the existence of the *Conscious Presence* within you. I will show you that the gate to *Heaven*, to *Eternity*, awaits you right at this very moment. In fact, you don't have to leave earth to experience it as you might have once thought. Through my experiences of Being Present with God and His wisdom and teachings, I have come to understand that the Bible is full of esoteric meaning; a deeper, hidden understanding that requires insight; the literal understanding of the words is just the first layer. God's Presence within you was never intended to be a mystery, and Eternal life is to be experienced now, in this Present moment of life's only reality. Your life's intended purpose was predestined before you were ever born. It has always existed deep within you, ready to be revealed; you just have to come into an awareness of it.

This is a book of wisdom and a practical guide to awaken your mind to *your true identity*, your inspired purpose and life's calling through the *renewing of your mind*, an *inner transformation*. I would like to offer you an opportunity to experience this same Spiritual awakening that I have experienced; an enlightenment of your mind that allows you to find your true self. I would like to show you the gate that unlocks your imprisoned mind to a pathway of self-discovery and transformation: a revelation so profound, the human mind cannot rationalize it; a Spiritual awakening within you that takes you from this world into the reality of another. If you have come from a place of brokenness, deep hurt, mental darkness, fear, and anxiety of the unknown, then this book is for you! Or if you have found yourself seeking a deeper Spiritual connection, a greater purpose found in the calling or drawing inward that life has for you, then this book is also for you!

How to Use This Book

I have decided to include some of my personal writings of wisdom when in the Presence of God throughout this manuscript. These are in capitalized headings inserted after each subchapter's narrative and are written either from the Holy Spirit's point of view (in which case the text is italicized) or from my point of view. In any case, both stem from the sessions of inspired wisdom and insight. The capitalized first person singular (*My, Me, Mine*) refers to God's Spirit, and the lowercase first person singular is myself. I have also included Scripture references in italics after each subchapter (sometimes I have added my own **emphasis** using boldface). These are the verses that came to me as I listened to God, which gave me further understanding of the wisdom I was receiving from Him.

I recommend reading this book in a quiet place away from life's distractions, and taking periods to reflect or meditate on the inspiration with writing tools in hand. With a clear and awake mind, having surrendered all thoughts, just listening and observing, wait patiently with full expectation of inspired thoughts of wisdom to flow within your awareness. Allow God, who is in you, to be your only teacher. He will, with certain conviction, bring the truth to your awareness, bathing you in wondrous revelation. I fully encourage you to write down the thoughts of wisdom and understanding that He gives you while in His Presence. May you become enlightened and delighted with the awareness of His Presence found in you! May you grow in deep desire to know Him, to seek Him, and to love Him above all else. Then the God of love will awaken you and reveal to you many wonderful things you have not yet known.

> Think over what I say, for the Lord will give you understanding in everything. (2 Timothy 2:7)

Chapter 1

The Kingdom of God, the Presence of Life— *It Is within You!*

Chapter 1.1

God Is Spirit—The Conscious Life Force Energy within You

The Spirit of God is of such great wonder. How can anyone ever know all of life's vastness and beauty? Its existence endures forever.

God, the Spirit, the Life Force Energy Within

God is Spirit, the existence or presence of a nonphysical inner being, the life force energy within you. Spirit is English for the Latin word *spiritus,* which means "breath." God, the Spirit or breath, is the conscious life flow energy that is present or manifested in all living things. This life flow essence is your very being, the existence of your aliveness in this moment. Through your consciousness or awareness of your breath of life, you are in Him, in God, through your awareness of living, moving, and having your being. This conscious life flow energy, your breath of life, is what sustains you to be in existence.

This nonphysical life force energy within you is a steady stream of consciousness. It is infinite intelligence, the Creator of all things living. It is the Father of all creation, for nothing that is living exists without the sustaining life force within it. This life force energy is unified and whole; it is the universal power that creates the action of aliveness and the moving of all things living. You are here in this moment of time, in existence, through the manifesting power of the life force energy that permeates you. The Spirit or your breath is God's presence within. This is just as Jesus demonstrated to His disciples by bringing them into this awareness of His breath when He had breathed on them and declared, "Receive the Holy Spirit."

The Name of God: A Name Which Cannot Be Spoken but Expressed through Your Awareness of the Breath

The Bible was written in three ancient languages: Hebrew and Aramaic in the Old Testament and Greek in the New Testament. It is said that the Jubilee Bible is the closest to the exact translation from Hebrew to English. In Exodus 3:14, when Moses asks God for His name to tell the sons of Israel, as rendered by that version, God answers, "I AM THAT I AM…. Thus shalt thou say unto the sons of Israel: I AM (YHWH) has sent me unto you." The Hebrew language, the language of Moses, the author of Exodus, is made up of only consonants with no vowels. Consonants are articulated by speech sounds in which the vocal track is partially or completely closed but the breath is forced to pronounce. Thus it is said that YHWH can be sounded with the inhalation breath of *YH* and exhaling the breath with a sound of *WH*. *Yahweh* is the English word for God, having added the vowels *a* and *e.*

Become consciously aware of your breath, the Holy Spirit, the presence of the life force energy that sustains your very existence of being alive in this moment. Become awakened to the vitality of your inner being, the manifesting Spirit within. Know that you are one with the manifesting presence of life, one with Spirit, through a conscious awareness of your breath! Through the focus of your breath, your mind has returned to a present state of awareness to life in the now. You are not separate from this life force energy, for without it, you would cease to exist. Through this conscious awareness of your aliveness, you are aware of the flow of life that exists within you: the Spirit of God—Yahweh! The Kingdom of God is found in a present state of mind because you are aware of the manifesting inner presence of aliveness, this life force that is within you! You are the very being of aliveness, the very being of the manifestation of God, of life itself.

We are born out of the sustaining existence of life, the creating energy flow that gives us our aliveness, our very being. The Creator, *life*, is the originator of all things living, and it gives us our presence of existence. Our very awareness to our conscious breath is the flow, the grace of the Spirit, within us. Through our breath, we are consciously aware of life's abiding presence, the very nature of the existence of life within us. It is an awareness through the appreciation of our aliveness in being one with life itself.

WE ARE BORN OF THE CREATOR, THE EXISTENCE OF LIFE ITSELF

Why, oh why, Lord, do we come into this world by Your creative being, Your existing life flow that sustains us, only to completely seek all things outside the awareness of Your presence? We are born into a physical world that seeks an outer false sense of awareness, a false reality that leads our minds astray; we exist yet have no awareness of Your very presence within. Every minute that we are *unconscious*, a mind that has no awareness of life's presence in the moment, we struggle with the truth and reality of life's existence. We fall away from Your very presence, our awareness to life itself. Through our mind's false self-awareness, we look away to seek more beyond You, yet nothing exists beyond the presence of life itself. In our mind's seeking and doing beyond life's present moment, we have attached ourselves to a false reality and have fallen away from Your presence of being.

Let us come back to our true selves, which are found only in our awareness of aliveness, our *breath of life*, life's abiding presence!

WELCOME THE SPIRIT THROUGH YOUR AWARENESS

Are you a host to the Spirit of God? Shall you welcome the presence of life into your consciousness and give Him a home? Shall you greet Him with praise and worship and offer up your best serving wine? Shall He come dine with you at your very own feast? Do you welcome the God of hosts, providing shelter to the Most High? For He will come sit with you! And He shall abide in you, your awareness to the very existence of aliveness! Surely life has revealed itself to you! Are you not aware of your very breath of life? Your innermost being, life itself? Then you have welcomed the Spirit, and you have welcomed life in your awareness of it. Come to a present state of mind to experience the presence of God!

$\mathcal{T}$HE TEMPLE OF GOD

For you are the temple to hold My life force within! Do you not see that it is I who sustains your very existence? Come rest in My presence, your consciousness! Be aware of the life flow that is within you. Come to your quiet place of solitude. Leave the world behind, and set your mind on Me! Quiet your thoughts now, and surrender to Me! I will enter your consciousness, your awareness of this moment. I will enter and make My presence known to you. Fully aware, we shall become one, for I AM life, and you have surrendered to My existence in the here and now. Your temple, your earthly vessel, is My temple to hold life itself. Come worship the life within you! Here I am, waiting for you.

The existence of God's presence has always been in you and in all! For out of its energy, you have been made.

$\mathcal{L}$IFE FLOW: YOUR VERY BEING

Your very being of aliveness is the Spirit of God within you! Are you not aware of the sustaining power, your inner being? Give reverence to the life flow within, the presence of the breath of life, the very nature of Spirit! Be aware of the manifestation of life that moves in and through you! For out of life is your very existence in this moment!

Allow the Spirit of God to overtake you; become alive in your knowledge of life itself. Become one with its ease and flow that permeates you!

Cease to resist this moment of awareness by surrendering to Spirit's presence, the breath of life, and its energy of your being of aliveness!

Surrender to the aliveness within you! For this is the Kingdom of God. Become consciously aware of living in this moment! You are one with the Spirit of life.

Allow God, the life force, to manifest within your awareness, overcoming you in the fullness of life itself. Simply surrender to the breath of life that is found in you to come into presence! God is in all and through all, and we are the vessels to hold life itself!

The Kingdom of God is a present, fully awakened state of mind. Be a present witness to the breath, the life force energy within you and all around you.

SPIRIT MANIFESTATION

Caught up in the awareness of My Spirit, you are fully alive in Me, My presence that is within you! Encouraged and empowered, you are filled with My Spirit. As you remain in the awareness of Me, you witness the manifesting presence of life that is within! You are fully aware of this moment of My manifesting Spirit, and you know that it is I who empowers you, who uplifts you do My will. It is My power, the existence of life, that moves and gives you being in this given moment. I am a God who manifests within you! I am your breath of existence; I am the giver of all life.

$\mathcal{G}$OD IS SPIRIT

*Or do you not know that **your body is a temple of the Holy Spirit within you**, **whom you have from God**? (1 Corinthians 6:19)*

> ***Where can I go from Your Spirit?***
> ***Or where can I flee from Your presence?***
> *(Psalm 139:7 NIV)*

*That according to the riches of his glory he may grant you to be strengthened with power through **his Spirit in your inner being**. (Ephesians 3:16)*

*And the dust returns to the earth as it was, and **the spirit returns to God who gave it**. (Ecclesiastes 12:7)*

$\mathcal{S}$PIRIT IS THE BREATH OF LIFE

> *Thus says God, the LORD,*
> > *who created the heavens and stretched them out,*
> > *who spread out the earth and what comes from it,*
> ***who gives breath to the people** on it*
> > ***and spirit** to those who walk in it …. (Isaiah 42:5)*

> ***The Spirit of God** has made me,*
> > ***and the breath** of the Almighty **gives me life**.*
> > *(Job 33:4)*

*Then the LORD God formed a man from the dust of the ground and **breathed into his nostrils the breath of life**, and the man **became a living being**. (Genesis 2:7)*

> ***As long as my breath is in me**,*
> > *and **the spirit of God is in my nostrils** ….*
> > *(Job 27:3)*

*And when he had said this, **he breathed on them** and said to them, "**Receive the Holy Spirit**." (John 20:22)*

$\mathcal{T}$HE SPIRIT, THE BREATH, IS THE CREATOR OF ALL THINGS LIVING. YOUR BREATH IS THE EXISTENCE OF THE NONPHYSICAL BEING, THE CONSCIOUS LIFE FORCE WITHIN YOU!

Worthy are you, our Lord and God,
*   to receive glory and honor and power,*
***for you created all things**,*
*   and by **your will they existed and were***
*   **created**. (Revelation 4:11)*

Have you not known? Have you not heard?
The LORD *is **the everlasting** God,*
*   the **Creator** of the ends of the earth.*
He does not faint or grow weary;
*   his understanding is unsearchable. (Isaiah 40:28)*

***One God and Father of all**, who is over all and **through all and in all**. (Ephesians 4:6)*

*For "**In him we live and move and have our being**"; as even some of your own poets have said, "For we are indeed his offspring." (Acts 17:28)*

$\mathcal{T}$HE NAME OF GOD, THE SPIRIT OR BREATH OF EXISTENCE, YHWH, CANNOT BE SPOKEN BUT EXPRESSED THROUGH THE AWARENESS OF YOUR BREATH

***And God answered unto Moses**, I AM THAT I AM. And he said, Thus shalt thou say unto the sons of Israel: **I AM (YHWH)** has sent me unto you. (Exodus 3:14 JUB)*

> *Praise Yah!*
>> *Praise **Yahweh's** name!*
>> *Praise him, you servants of **Yahweh**,*
> ***you who stand in Yahweh's house**,*
>> *in the courts of our God's house. (Psalm 135:1–2 WEB)*

Chapter 1.2

The Presence of Life—The Essence of All Things Living

The Kingdom of God Is within Your Midst—The Mind's Awareness to the Spirit Within

Through the study of the brain we know that *within its midst* lies the mind. Unlike the brain's physical structure, the mind is nonphysical and a separate entity of its own. The mind consists of your thoughts and Consciousness: your awareness to life's Presence and its existence within you and in all things living. Consciousness is the sense of soul, your awareness or intuitiveness to the *inner Being* of aliveness within you. The knowledge of *the Kingdom of God* is through your Consciousness, or through the mind's *light of awareness* of the free flow energy that permeates you to give you your aliveness and existence of Being. Within the mind, within Conscious awareness, we are brought into a Present state of Being, One with life in the now.

It is interesting to note that René Descartes, a French philosopher and scientist, regarded the pineal gland, a tiny structure within the brain, as the "principal seat of the soul." Our Consciousness, or our mind's awareness to life's inner Being within us, is the Kingdom of God. As Jesus said, what good would it be if someone had gained the whole world yet forfeited their soul? Forfeiting your soul is not having the mind's awareness to God's Presence, or a Present state of mind, to life in the now. As Jesus proclaimed, the Kingdom of God is within your midst. Consciousness is your awareness to the inner Being that is within you—that which gives you your aliveness in this Present moment of your existence. You were created with a Conscious awareness to the Presence of life within you, your Oneness with it. This is your *God Consciousness*, your awareness to life's abiding Presence within.

The pineal gland, shaped like a pine cone, rests between the two brain hemispheres and represents a photoreceptor or "simple eye." The pineal gland is often referred to as the "pineal eye," "single eye," "the parietal," or "the third eye." It is your state of awareness, the alert and awake mind, your Consciousness to the Presence of life in this moment. In the book of Genesis, Jacob refers to the place where he had seen God face to face, and he called that place Peniel. In Matthew, Jesus explains that the light of the body *(the light of awareness* or *Consciousness)* is the eye *(the third eye pineal eye).* And "if therefore thine eye be single"—some translations have used the word *simple* (the pineal eye)—then "thy whole body shall be full of light" (*the light of awareness*; see Matthew 6:22).

In the Metaphorical *Garden* of the Mind Lies the Metaphorical *Tree of Life*, the Conscious Awareness to Life's Presence

As I began to study the book of Genesis in my meditation with God, and in particular, *God's creation of man*, it was clear to me that the writer is using esoteric wisdom to reveal the hidden meaning of man's creation. *Earth* is used as a metaphor for the brain structure. A *garden* is used as the metaphor to describe the anatomy of the cerebrum or cortex, which is the largest part of the brain associated with higher brain function of thought and action. We see that God breathed life into the man and placed him in another garden eastward, called the *Garden of Eden*, which represents the mind. The Garden of Eden is revealed as the place of Consciousness, for within the *Garden* was planted the *Tree of Life* or the awareness to life's Presence. *The Tree of Life* is the Conscious awareness to the Presence of life itself, found within *Eden* or the mind.

We then see that the writer continues with the analogy of the *whole larger garden*, where other trees have been planted, as the cerebrum. A river, which is used as a metaphor for the life force energy within us, leaves *Eden* (the mind) to water the rest of the *garden* (cerebrum). *The river,* or life force energy, sections or parts the larger *garden* (cerebrum) into four heads.

In Genesis 2:10–14, we see the *head parts* that each river divides into within the garden. This is their Hebrew translation:

1. Pishon—Increase or full flowing
2. Gihon—Bursting forth or gushing
3. Hiddekel—Swift or darting
4. Euphrates—Sweet or fruitful

Now we see the four main cerebrum sections or lobes, with their corresponding primary functions:

1. Frontal lobe—problem solving
2. Parietal lobe—body orientation
3. Temporal lobe—memory
4. Occipital lobe—visual reception

It is evident here that the writer is metaphorically describing the cerebral lobes and their primary functions as a large garden parted into four *head parts* (following the King James and Jubilee rendering) by rivers that describe the land that they occupy. As told by the writer, we can eat from any tree of the garden that stems out from Eden. That is, we can experience life through any lobe of the cerebrum, the brain's higher functioning area, through our mind's Present state of Conscious awareness.

Now let's put together the whole allegory by using the biblical metaphors with the reality of life's existence, its Presence within you: In the Garden (cerebrum) lies eastward another garden called Eden (mind). Within the midst of the Garden of Eden (mind) lies the Tree of Life (Consciousness)—having the awareness of life's existence; and out of the mind flow the rivers (life force energy) which separate the Garden (cerebrum) into four head parts (four cerebral lobes). Through our Consciousness, our awareness to life's existence (the Tree of Life), we can we can eat from any tree of the Garden (cerebrum, the brain's higher functioning areas) to experience life's Presence in its fullness.

Coming before *the throne of God* is positioning your mind to a Present state of Conscious awareness to life's Presence; having a mind that is Present, fully aware of its surroundings in the here and now, this Present moment. And if we are fully Present of mind, we can experience each of the higher brain functions with fullness of Conscious clarity. This is God Consciousness: having the awareness of life's Presence within us, fully in the now of Being One with it.

Life Is the Heart of All Things

The central, innermost part of something, or its *heart*, is its vital essence. It is the nucleus or core of something that gives it its identity. Within the heart or the inner essence of all living things is *God Consciousness*—our awareness to life's Presence—and *Spirit*, the life force energy that brings our moving and Being into existence. This is our true identity, our core of what sustains us: having our breath of life, our Being and aliveness in this moment. Our heart, the mind's Consciousness, is the essence of who we are. We are alive because of the life force energy that sustains us in our vitality, and without it we would not exist in this moment of time.

We can therefore say that *the heart of man*, or *his essence*, is the mind's Conscious awareness to life's Presence. We are Consciously aware in this moment that we are alive and have our Being. It is through our Conscious awareness that the life force energy is known to us. We know it is our *innermost part*, our essence of aliveness. As Scripture teaches, God, or the Conscious life force energy, formed our *inward parts* inside our mother's womb. And *out of man's heart flow the springs of life*, his Conscious awareness to life's Presence, its energy flow within.

The Kingdom of God, the Presence of life, is found within you. The Kingdom is your mind's Present state of Conscious awareness to life itself.

Be alert, awake, and aware of the ever-Present flowing life force within. Become fully aware of life's Being that flows in and through you! For out of its nature, you exist!

THE ALERT AND PRESENT MIND—THE DRIVING FORCE OF CONSCIOUSNESS

Be aware in this moment to My Presence within!

Surrender to a mind that is Present, fully awake in its awareness of Being One with life. Let your mind drift into Me, the energy and flow of life that sustains you. Have you no awareness of My movement, My grace that upholds your very existence? The knowing of My Presence is through your Consciousness, your mind's awareness of My Being, within. Give reverence to the life that is found in you. Your very breath is My life force. For I enter within you, your Consciousness.

Be of full mind in awareness of My existence within, conforming your awareness to the Oneness of life itself.

SURRENDER TO LIFE

Surrender to the Presence of life itself! Surrender to its natural flow within you and around you. For this is the *will* of God, the power and intent to life's natural flow. Your mind has been renewed to an awareness of the Presence of life within you, for you are One with life's existence, having knowledge of its energy and flow that sustains you. You have surrendered to your awareness of Spirit, the life flow within! Your mind has become alert to your breath, your Conscious internal flow of life. You have conformed to the very nature of life itself when you have become fully alert to its abiding Presence within. Surrender to the Kingdom's Present state of mind and gain awareness to life's abiding Presence within!

$\mathcal{T}$HE EXISTENCE OF LIFE, THE CREATOR OF ALL THINGS, IS WITHIN YOU; IT IS THROUGH THE MIND'S CONSCIOUS AWARENESS OF THE SOUL, THE ESSENCE OR INNER BEING OF ALIVENESS.

Then the Lord *God formed a man from the dust of the ground and **breathed into his nostrils the breath of life**, and the man became **a living being**. (Genesis 2:7 NIV)*

> **For you created my inmost being**;
>   *you knit me together in my mother's womb.*
>   *(Psalm 139:13 NIV)*

*Being asked by the Pharisees when the kingdom of God would come, he answered them, "**The kingdom of God is not coming in ways that can be observed**, nor will they say, '**Look, here it is!**' or '**There!**' for behold, **the kingdom of God is in the midst of you**." (Luke 17:20–21)*

*That according to the riches of his glory he may grant you to be strengthened with power through **his Spirit** in **your inner being** .... (Ephesians 3:16)*

*For I delight in the law of **God**, in **my inner being** .... (Romans 7:22)*

> *Behold, you delight in truth in the **inward being**,*
>   *and you **teach me wisdom** in the **secret heart**.*
>   *(Psalm 51:6)*

*Have I not commanded you? Be strong and courageous. Do not be frightened, and do not be dismayed, **for the Lord your God is with you wherever you go**. (Joshua 1:9)*

*Do not be conformed to this world, but **be transformed by the renewal of your mind**, that by testing **you may discern what** *is the will of God*, *what is good and acceptable and perfect.* *(Romans 12:2)*

*For those who live according to the flesh set their minds on the things of the flesh, but **those who live according to the Spirit set their minds on the things of the Spirit**. For to set the mind on the flesh is death, **but to set the mind on the Spirit is life** and peace. (Romans 8:5–6)*

> ***Keep your heart with all vigilance**,*
> *for **from it flow the springs of life**.*
> *(Proverbs 4:23)*

***For what will it profit a man if he gains the whole world** and **forfeits his soul**? Or what shall a man give in return for his soul? (Matthew 16:26)*

$\mathcal{T}$HE LIGHT OF CONSCIOUS AWARENESS; THE SINGLE EYE, THE PINEAL.

***The light** of the body **is the eye**: **if therefore thine eye be single**, **thy whole body shall be full of light**. (Matthew 6:22 NIV)*

*So Jacob called the name of the place **Peniel**, saying, "**For I have seen God face to face**, and yet my life has been delivered." (Genesis 32:30)*

*Therefore, knowing the fear of the Lord, we persuade others. But **what we are is known to God**, and **I hope it is known also to your conscience**. (2 Corinthians 5:11)*

$\mathcal{A}$ COLLECTIVE OR ONE GOD CONSCIOUSNESS IN ALL.

***And I will give** them **one heart**, and **a new spirit I will put within them**. (Ezekiel 11:19)*

$\mathcal{T}$HE ALLEGORICAL BIBLICAL CREATION OF MAN:

$\mathcal{T}$HE PRESENCE OF LIFE (GOD) FOUND IN MAN EXISTS WITHIN THE MIND (EDEN).

And the LORD ***God*** *had planted **a garden eastward in Eden**; and there **he put the man whom he had formed**. (Genesis 2:8 KJV)*

$\mathcal{T}$HE TREE OF LIFE WITHIN THE MIDST OF THE GARDEN IS OUR MIND'S CONSCIOUS AWARENESS TO LIFE'S PRESENCE IN THE NOW.

And out of the ground made the LORD *God to grow every tree that is pleasant to the sight and good for food, **the tree of life also in the midst of the garden** …. (Genesis 2:9 KJV)*

$\mathcal{T}$HE RIVER IS LIFE'S FREE FLOW ENERGY THAT LEAVES THE MIND (EDEN) TO WATER OR BRING CONSCIOUS AWARENESS TO THE FOUR AREAS OF THE CEREBRUM OF THE BRAIN (GARDEN).

*And a **river went out of Eden** to **water the garden**; and from thence it was **parted**, and **became into four heads**. (Genesis 2:10 KJV)*

$\mathcal{T}$HE FIRST SECTION OF THE CEREBRUM IS THE FRONTAL (FIRST) LOBE (PISON), WHICH ENCOMPASSES THE WHOLE FRONT SECTION OF THE CORTEX. THE METAPHOR STATES IT ENCOMPASSES THE WHOLE LAND OF THE PEOPLE.

*The name of **the first is Pison**: that is it which **compasseth the whole land of Havilah**, where there is gold …. (Genesis 2:11 KJV)*

$\mathcal{T}$HE SECOND SECTION OF THE CEREBRUM IS THE PARIETAL LOBE (GIHON), WHICH ALSO ENCOMPASES THE WHOLE LEFT AND RIGHT OF THE CORTEX; THE METAPHOR SUGGESTS IT TOO IS THE SAME, ENCOMPASSING THE WHOLE.

*And the name of **the second river** is **Gihon**: the same is it that **compasseth the whole land of Ethiopia**. (Genesis 2:13 KJV)*

$\mathcal{T}$HE THIRD SECTION OF THE CEREBRUM IS THE TEMPORAL LOBE FOUND TO THE EAST OF THE CORTEX (HIDDEKEL).

*And the name of **the third river is Hiddekel**: that is it which goeth toward the **east** of Assyria. (Genesis 2:14 KJV)*

$\mathcal{T}$HE FOURTH SECTION OF THE CEREBRUM IS THE OCCIPITAL LOBE (EUPHRATES).

*And **the fourth river** is **Euphrates**. (Genesis 2:14 KJV)*

$\mathcal{W}$E WERE CREATED TO EXIST WITHIN OUR MIND'S CONSCIOUS AWARENESS TO LIFE'S PRESENCE IN THE NOW.

*And the LORD **God took the man**, and **put him into the garden of Eden** to dress it and to keep it. (Genesis 2:15 KJV)*

$\mathcal{A}$ND THROUGH OUR MIND'S CONSCIOUS AWARENESS WE EXPERIENCE LIFE'S FULLNESS THROUGH THE HIGHER FUNCTIONING PART OF OUR BRAIN.

*And the LORD God commanded the man, saying, **Of every tree of the garden thou mayest freely eat** …. (Genesis 2:16 KJV)*

Chapter 1.3

Enlightenment—Your Conscious Awareness to Life's Presence

In light of your awareness of the truth of your essence of existence, you have become enlightened to the Conscious life force energy that permeates your very Being. Having awareness through the mind's eye, or the internal knowing of God's Presence within, you have been renewed. Through a Present state of mind of being Consciously aware of the existence of life's Presence within you and all around you, you have awakened your mind in this moment. Life's Presence is within all living things. It is your sustaining breath and heartbeat. It is your vitality for Being Present in this moment of existence. In the mind's renewal, you are now the observing mind through your awareness of life within you and around you.

Your awakened mind is the drawing of your attention inward to the awareness of the Spirit, the flow of the life force energy that is within you! Spirit or life flow energy has always been *interwoven in your innermost parts.* You are awakened to your Consciousness of God's Presence, the inner Being that sustains your very existence. Your mind has been set on Spirit, and you have been drawn into the Presence of life's existence within you. Your mind is in a state of Presence as it has become awakened and aware to your inner Being of aliveness.

ℰNLIGHTENMENT—OPENING YOUR MIND TO AWARENESS

Can the slave open the door to his enclosure? Or the prisoner open the door to his cell? Surely not! The master holds the key to such things. Come into the awareness of My Being, the reality of life's existence within you! Come into My Presence through your Conscious awareness of My aliveness within you!

The Conscious awareness of God's Spirit that is moving freely within you has renewed your mind. For you have been brought into the light of awareness of life, the truth of its reality. The Presence of life is within you, moving freely about, sustaining you in this moment of your awareness to it. Surrender to the existence of life, the Spirit's vitality within, through a fully Present state of mind. This is your enlightenment: your awareness of the Spirit of God, the life force that is active in you.

You are the stream of Consciousness: your awareness of the essence of life flow energy within.

𝒴OU HAVE BEEN BROUGHT INTO THE LIGHT OF AWARENESS TO LIFE'S PRESENCE. WE HAVE THE LIGHT OF LIFE!

Having the eyes of your hearts enlightened, *that you may know what is the hope to which he has called you, what are the riches of his* **glorious inheritance** *in the saints …. (Ephesians 1:18)*

> *For you have delivered my soul from death,*
> *yes, my feet from falling,*
> **that I may walk before God**
> **in the light of life**. *(Psalm 56:13)*

They must hold the mystery of the **faith with a clear conscience**. *(1 Timothy 3:9)*

You are the light of the world. *A city set on a hill cannot be hidden. (Matthew 5:14)*

But if we **walk in the light**, **as he is in the light**, *we have fellowship with one another, and the blood of Jesus his Son cleanses us from all sin. (1 John 1:7)*

But whoever does what is true **comes to the light**, *so that it may be clearly seen that* **his works have been carried out in God**. *(John 3:21)*

Chapter 1.4

Eternal Life Is Living in the Present

The Human Mind's State of Awareness to Experience Life in the Present or Presence of It

The Eternal life, *the One true God*, is your knowing or awareness to life's Presence within you. *Eternal* is defined as having no beginning or end, forever existing; it is an endless existence outside all relations of time. God, the life force energy, the Creator of all things, is eternal. Life is an eternal, nonphysical, ever-Present essence that is sustaining you into existence.

The Kingdom of God is our mind's Conscious awareness to the Presence of life that exists within and all around us. The Kingdom of God is a Present state of mind that directly perceives or experiences life through its awareness of it. As Jesus spoke, the Kingdom of God is *at hand*; it is now accessible. And behold, the *favorable time is now*, the time of salvation, *is now*. The Kingdom of God, or our mind's Conscious awareness to life's Presence, is to be experienced *now*. The Present is what you clearly see and experience now. Life's reality of existence is found in our mind's awareness to its Presence in the now. Eternal life, or the Kingdom of God, is our mind's Present state of awareness or perspective to life in the now occurring.

The mind's Present state of awareness is what lies between the past as a memory, and the future as an expectation. Both past and future states of mind are illusions to the reality of Presence, the awareness of life's reality of existence at hand or in the now.

In your awareness to life's inner Presence, its very essence of you, you realize you *are* the Conscious eternal life force; you are one with its manifesting Presence within. You are one with life in your awareness of it, *which is the light of life.* If you remain in the state of a Conscious awareness to life's Presence, then you are living in the Present, the now of life's only eternal existence.

No life, *no thing* exists outside of the mind's Present state of awareness, for life is only found within the mind that is Present with it. The mind's positioning, or its experiencing of the past and the future states while existing, are illusions to the reality or truth of life's only existence. These illusory states lead your mind away from its awareness to the Presence of life itself. To *gain Eternal life*, one must live in the Present, forgiving the past and trusting for the future, remaining in the now, this Present moment of time.

My Presence is Eternal. It is life that exists in your Being in the here and now. I AM your inner Being of aliveness! I AM your Conscious awareness to what is—life in this moment! I AM your gift of vitality, I AM your life force energy within you!

Become aware right now of the life that exists within you and all around you! Enter the light of awareness of Eternity.

$\mathcal{M}$EET ME HERE IN THIS PLACE

Oh, You who have no mercy, you cry! Oh, You, who have no love for me! Oh Lord, why do You forsake me? you ask. Oh Lord, why have You left me to suffer? But then I say, Dear child, I have not left you! No! I AM forever here. Yet you hide your face from Me, and you refuse to meet Me. You have set out to seek something beyond life, beyond My Presence. So I ask you, child, why have you forsaken Me so? Surely, I AM, but you do not seek Me here in this place. No, you allow your mind to stray, resisting what is: life in the Present.

Surrender your mind to the awareness of Me, the life flow energy that is your very Being. Become alive in the now, the reality of life. Seek Me, the life that exists in you, and you shall become Consciously aware of My Presence. I AM a God who does not hide but reveals Himself, for I AM life, here in the Presence of existence. Shall you hide your self from Me? This Presence of Being alive? Then come, come meet Me in the place of your mind's surrender to the awareness of Being. Turn your mind from seeking all else outside of My Presence, and do not resist life in this moment. Become One with life, with Me, for nothing exists beyond it!

$\mathcal{E}$TERNAL LIFE IS FOUND WITHIN THE MIND'S CONSCIOUS AWARENSS TO ITS INNER PRESENCE. IT IS FOUND IN THE PRESENT MIND, OR PRESENCE OF IT.

And this is eternal life, that they know you, the only true God, and Jesus Christ whom you have sent. (John 17:3)

*For the wages of sin is death, but **the free gift of God is eternal life** in Christ Jesus our Lord. (Romans 6:23)*

*Truly, truly, I say to you, whoever hears my word and **believes him who sent me has eternal life**. He does not come into judgment, but has **passed from death to life**. (John 5:24)*

$\mathcal{A}$ CONSCIOUS AWARENESS OF GOD, THE ETERNAL LIFE FORCE WITHIN YOU.

*For "**In him we live and move and have our being**"; as even some of your own poets have said, "**For we are indeed his offspring**." (Acts 17:28)*

$\mathcal{E}$TERNAL LIFE FOUND WITHIN YOUR CONSCIOUS AWARENESS TO LIFE'S PRESENCE (HEART).

*He has made everything beautiful in its time. Also, **he has put eternity into man's heart**, yet so that he cannot find out what God has done from the beginning to the end. (Ecclesiastes 3:11)*

$\mathcal{G}$OD'S PRESENCE IS FOUND IN THE MIND THAT IS PRESENT TO LIFE IN THE NOW, THE REALITY OF LIFE'S ONLY EXISTENCE.

*From that time Jesus began to preach, saying, "**Repent, for the kingdom of heaven is at hand**." (Matthew 4:17)*

*And proclaim as you go, saying, "**The kingdom of heaven is at hand**." (Matthew 10:7)*

*For he says, "In a favorable time I listened to you, and in a day of salvation I have helped you." Behold, **now is the favorable time**; behold, **now is the day of salvation**. (2 Corinthians 6:2)*

> ***You make known to me the path of life**;*
> > ***in your presence** there is fullness of joy;*
> > *at your right hand are pleasures forevermore.*
> > *(Psalm 16:11)*

*And he said, "**My presence will go with you**, and I will give you rest." (Exodus 33:14)*

*That times of refreshing may come **from the presence of the Lord**, and that he may send the Christ appointed for you, Jesus …. (Acts 3:20)*

Chapter 2

Your Real Identity—
The Truth of Who You Are

Chapter 2.1

We Are Made in His Imagination, Having the Likeness of Our Creator

Your Creation and Essence

You were fearfully and wonderfully made through the One Consciousness Creator. Your sustaining essence, your inner Being of aliveness, is the Conscious life flow energy, Infinite Intelligence, the Creator of all things living. Knit together in your mother's womb, you were made in His image, His imagination. Having been made in His likeness, you are the manifesting essence of life itself.

You are One with life, One with God, through your Conscious awareness of the inner Being that allows for your existence. You are the powerful creative imagination within. You are all gods, as Jesus declared, and that is your true-identity, the truth of who you are.

When you surrender your mind to a Present state of awareness to life, you are One with the inner Being of life's existence. God manifests through you!

Be aware of Me, My energy that sustains you! For I AM life, and in your Present awareness you have become One with Me, One with life!

Sons and Daughters of Life's Essence

We are all One with God in our awareness of Him and His life energy that flows through us. We all have God within us, His Spirit, His life flow energy that sustains us. We are all One with life, having existence through its very nature of Being. We are all connected as One with the life force energy within us. We are the very reflection, the very essence and likeness of the nature of life. It is our vitality of existence, our identity.

You have become One with the essence or likeness of life, its very existence. You are My likeness, the life energy that flows through you! For this is My very nature, the breath of your vitality as you see, you are My very nature, life in existence of Me!

𝒴OU WERE CREATED BY GOD, THE CONSCIOUS LIFE FLOW ENERGY WITHIN THAT SUSTAINS YOU; YOU ARE GOD'S MANIFESTING PRESENCE.

*Then God said, "**Let us make man in our image, after our likeness**. And let them have dominion over the fish of the sea and over the birds of the heavens and over the livestock and over all the earth and over every creeping thing that creeps on the earth."*

> *So **God created man in his own image,***
> > ***in the image of God he created him;***
> > ***male and female he created them**. (Genesis 1:26–27)*

> *For **you formed my inward parts**;*
> > ***you knitted me together in my mother's womb**.*
> *I praise you, for **I am fearfully and wonderfully made**.*
> > *Wonderful are your works;*
> > ***my soul knows it very well**. (Psalm 139:13–14)*

***And we all, with unveiled face**, beholding the glory of the **Lord**, are being **transformed into the same image** from one degree of glory to another. **For this comes from the Lord who is the Spirit**. (2 Corinthians 3:18)*

> *I said, "**You are gods**,*
> > *And all of you are **sons of the Most High**."*
> > *(Psalm 82:6 NIV)*

*Jesus answered them, "Has it not been written in your Law, '**I said, you are gods'**?" (John 10:34 NIV)*

> ***I will be a father to you**,*
> > *and **you will be My sons and daughters**,*
> > *says the Lord Almighty. (2 Corinthians 6:18 NIV)*

*In their case the god of this world **has blinded the minds of the unbelievers, to keep them from seeing the light** of the gospel of **the glory of Christ**, who is **the image of God**. (2 Corinthians 4:4)*

***He is the radiance of the glory of God** and the **exact imprint of his nature**, and he upholds the universe by the word of his power. (Hebrews 1:3)*

Chapter 2.2

We Are the Manifested Vessels of Life

The Vessel of Life's Essence

You are the external physical creation that holds the internal, nonphysical life force energy that flows within you. You are the medium, the channel, the holder, and the receiver of life. Your physical body that you acquire is the vehicle or vessel that carries the life flow energy within you. Your vessel manifests the very existence of life through it as it gives you the Being and moving in aliveness. You are the Conscious manifesting Presence within. You are God, you are One with life, in its expressing of itself through a human body form. In your mind's Present awareness to life's existence, you have become One with all there is, your true alignment with the inner Being. You are God expressing life through your earthly vessel.

You were created as My vessel, to hold My Presence of life within! Your earthly vessel is My home, where I exist. It is My Being that lives and moves in you, for I AM life, your very existence in this moment of Presence!

You are the vessel of the Presence of life! You allow Me to express my natural unfolding through you!

$\mathcal{W}$E ARE MANIFESTED VESSELS OF GOD; THE ESSENCE OR LIFE ENERGY THAT FLOWS THROUGH US.

*Or what agreement has the temple of God with idols? For **we are the temple of the living God**; just as God said,*

> *"**I will dwell in them** and walk among them;*
>   *and **I will be their God, and they shall be My***
>   ***people**." (2 Corinthians 6:16 NASB)*

*For by him all things were created, in heaven and on earth, visible and invisible, whether thrones or dominions or rulers or authorities—**all things were created through him and for him**. (Colossians 1:16)*

*Do you not know that **you are God's temple and** that **God's Spirit dwells in you**? If anyone destroys God's temple, God will destroy him. For God's temple is holy, **and you are that temple**. (1 Corinthians 3:16–17)*

***But we have this treasure in jars of clay, to show that the surpassing power belongs to God and not to us**. (2 Corinthians 4:7)*

***And I will give you a new heart**, and **a new spirit I will put within you**. And I will remove the heart of stone from your flesh and give you a heart of flesh. **And I will put my Spirit within you**, and cause you to walk in my statutes and be careful to obey my rules. (Ezekiel 36:26–27)*

*Or do you not know that **your body is a temple of the Holy Spirit within you**, whom you have from God? **You are not your own**, for you were bought with a price. (1 Corinthians 6:19–20)*

Built on the foundation of the apostles and prophets, Christ Jesus himself being the cornerstone, in whom the whole structure, being joined together, **grows into a holy temple in the Lord**. *In him you also are* **being built together into a dwelling place for God by the Spirit**. *(Ephesians 2:20–22)*

*F***or it is God who is at work in you**, *both* **to will and to work for His good pleasure**. *(Philippians 2:13 NASB)*

Chapter 2.3

You Are the Manifestation of God—The Alignment with Your True Identity

The Mind's Right Standing Position, its *Righteousness*, is a Present State of Awareness to Life

In your awareness to life's Presence within you, its flow of life force energy that sustains your moving and Being into existence, you become One with it. You become One with God, the Creator of all things living. You are the manifestation of God through your earthly vessel. You are the manifestation, the existence and reality of life's Presence within. In the awareness of your Oneness, you have come into an *agreement* or *alignment* with who you are: the manifestation of Consciousness itself. You are the manifesting Presence of God, the Consciousness within. Your mind's correct positioning, its right standing, or as the Bible teaches its *righteousness* because of belief; is one of a full Conscious awareness to the Presence of God within you, in this favorable time, the now of life's existence.

You have been transformed through your mind's renewal of a right positioning, one of awareness to life's existence within you and all around you. In your mind's positioning, you are in alignment with your true identity: God's manifestation through you. Your mind has come to a Present state of awareness to life in the now.

The Divine nature, this life flow within, is the common thread that connects us all! We are all One in life, as we are all the manifesting Presence of life itself. We are not a separate identity but become One with life itself when we surrender to our awareness of it! We become the Conscious awareness to simply Being One with life's Presence, found only in the now, the true reality of life.

Surrender to life; the mind's awakening to the Present awareness of all that is in the now.

$\mathcal{I}$ KNEW YOU BEFORE YOU WERE BORN

What a Divine Intelligent Creator You are, to manifest Yourself through every vessel You have made! You knew me before the world was made, of course! You knew me in my mother's womb, of course! As I am aware of You, You, dear life, are in me! I was always with You in eternity. For I AM life, I AM You, God, manifesting fully in Presence, fully alive in Consciousness! I AM life, I AM Being, I AM fully Consciously aware and Present in the now through the reality of Your sustaining existence!

Oh, Divine Creator, how intelligent You are! How could You, the existence of life, create a perfect masterpiece without dwelling in it? Without You, my life and Being, I no longer exist. But with You, the manifesting life within me, I exist! For I am awake to Your abiding Presence within! I am awake to the stirring of life that allows me to be Present, right now. I shall remain here in this Presence of aliveness and be aware of Your flow that is sustaining me!

$\mathcal{Y}$OU ARE ETERNAL SPIRIT, ETERNAL LIFE

Life is everlasting; it does not end but continues forever. Life is the Creator of the universe, the Creator of all things living! Life is the originator of all things, for nothing living exists without it.

You are One with life, the life force that is expressing itself through your earthly vessel. You are Eternal, you are the Being, the moving and existing in the mind's Present awareness of it. You are God, the manifesting life force flowing through your body. Allow your mind to surrender to the life force that is moving within you, to the awareness of Spirit, the breath. Come to the awareness life's Presence in the now. Absolutely nothing exists outside of Presence, for life is now, never ending and eternal.

Have your mind come into its alignment with Presence, for this is your right standing position, your true identity with life!

$\mathcal{R}$IGHTEOUSNESS THROUGH FAITH

Having believed in God, the life force energy that flows within you, is the mind's right standing position. You are One with God through your awareness of His Presence; you are *justified, you are right,* through your awareness; you are *righteousness*, the mind's right standing, in alignment, in union with, and in Oneness with the Presence of life itself. This is your *righteousness through faith!* Your mind's Conscious awareness to life's Presence in the now, this favorable time at hand, the now of the mind's salvation.

$\mathcal{W}$E ARE ONE WITH GOD, ONE WITH LIFE, THROUGH OUR AWARENESS OF ITS PRESENCE OF BEING WITHIN US. WE HAVE GAINED LIFE IN OUR AWARENESS TO IT!

Have we not all **one Father**? *Has not* **one God created us**? *Why then are we faithless to one another, profaning the covenant of our fathers? (Malachi 2:10)*

For in **one Spirit** *we were all baptized into one body—Jews or Greeks, slaves or free—and all were made to drink* **of one Spirit**. *(1 Corinthians 12:13)*

One God *and* **Father of all**, *who is over all and* **through all** *and* **in all**. *(Ephesians 4:6)*

$\mathcal{W}$E ARE IN UNION WITH LIFE, AND THIS IS OUR ALIGNMENT, OUR MIND'S RIGHT STANDING POSITION. WE ARE JUSTIFIED (RIGHTEOUS) IN OUR AWARENESS (BELIEF) TO LIFE'S PRESENCE IN THE NOW.

*For what does the Scripture say? "*** Abraham believed God***, and it was counted to him* **as righteousness**." *(Romans 4:3)*

For in it [the gospel] the **righteousness of God is revealed from faith for faith**, *as it is written, "*** The righteous shall live by faith**." *(Romans 1:17 NIV)*

Since **God is one**—*who will* **justify** *the circumcised* **by faith** *and the uncircumcised through faith. (Romans 3:30)*

Therefore, since we have been **justified by faith**, **we have peace with God** *through our Lord Jesus Christ. (Romans 5:1)*

And **be found in him**, **not having a righteousness of my own that comes from the law**, *but that which comes* **through faith** *in*

*Christ, **the righteousness from God that depends on faith** ....
(Philippians 3:9)*

***For we hold that one is justified by faith** apart from works of
the law. (Romans 3:28**)***

*And to the one who does not work but **believes in him** who
justifies the ungodly, his **faith is counted as righteousness** ....
(Romans 4:5)*

*And such were some of you. But you were washed, you were
sanctified, you were **justified** in the name of the Lord Jesus Christ
and **by the Spirit of our God**. (1 Corinthians 6:11)*

*And are **justified by his grace as a gift**, through the redemption
that is in Christ Jesus. (Romans 3:24)*

*So that **being justified by his grace** we might become **heirs**
according to the hope **of eternal life**. (Titus 3:7)*

**YOU SHALL KNOW OF GOD'S PRESENCE
THROUGH THE MIND'S RIGHT STANDING
POSITION; A PRESENT STATE OF AWARENESS
(AN AWAKENED STATE) TO LIFE IN THE NOW.**

*As for me, I shall **behold your face in righteousness**;
**when I awake, I shall be satisfied with your
likeness**. (Psalm 17:15)*

Chapter 2.4

Falling Away from the Presence of Life— The Birth of Self-Awareness

The Mind's Fall from a Conscious Present State of Awareness—God Consciousness

To reference the Bible and *man's falling away from God*, or the mind's falling away from a Conscious Present state of awareness; we will decipher the metaphors used within the analogy in the Book of Genesis.

In the Metaphorical *Garden* of the Mind Lies the Metaphorical *Tree of Knowledge of Good and Evil*

You were created to exist within the mind's Present state of awareness, God Consciousness, or the awareness to life's Presence in the now of reality. The *Tree of Life* in the metaphorical creation of man is the reference to the existence of life's Presence through the mind's Conscious awareness of it. Through our mind's Consciousness, the Tree of Life extends its branches of life force energy, *the living waters*, throughout the areas of the brain's higher functioning capabilities to experience the world around you.

Through the writer's analogy, we learn that within the midst of the Garden of Eden, the mind, there was also another tree, *The Tree of Knowledge of Good and Evil.* The Tree of Knowledge represents the introduction of a separate awareness to the mind, for we know that Adam and Eve had no *self-awareness* prior to this, yet remained in life's Presence (God Consciousness) freely, unashamed of their naked bodies. There was no self-awareness to realize that their bodies were unclothed.

If they were to eat the fruit from the Tree of Knowledge, they

41

would gain knowledge of both good and evil. That is, they would experience a separate awareness or knowledge other than what they had already known, God Consciousness or the mind's Present state of awareness to life. The *knowledge of good* is the mind's Present state of awareness of God's Presence or life found in the now of reality. The *knowledge of evil* is the separate awareness that is born out of a mind that has fallen from a Present state of awareness to a false self-awareness. For then we know, as Adam and Eve had eaten from this tree, they had gained knowledge (a separate self-awareness) of their nakedness and they became ashamed and hid themselves. This knowledge of self-awareness separates the mind from God Consciousness, or the awareness of life's reality of Presence found in the now, the Present state of mind.

The Deception: That the Reality of Life Exists Beyond a Present State of Mind

Through the deception of the *serpent*, a metaphor representing a temptation or desire, the seed was planted within their minds to seek an experience outside the Tree of Life or the Presence of life's only existence. This is the deception or illusion; a sense of false awareness within the mind, for no life exists beyond the reality of its Presence. We see that there was a desire to know what lies beyond the existence of life's Presence of the here and now, and the desire looked appealing enough that they succumbed to the temptation. Desire gives birth to sin, as the Bible denotes. That is, the mind that drifts from a present state of being to the seeking of a desire or something more than what is, has missed the mark (or sinned) to life's reality. The mind in its seeking or desiring for more has left the present state of life's existence. We see that Adam and Eve had given birth to a desire and had fallen or left the Presence of God, the awareness of life in that moment.

Through the Mind's Desire for More, a False or Separate Awareness is Born

Through the desire and temptation within our mind to seek something outside the reality of life's Presence, the now, we enter into a false or separate awareness to life's existence. We leave the mind's Present state of Conscious awareness, God Consciousness or the awareness of life's reality, and we enter into a death experience within the mind, for we are outside the Presence of life. We know that the reality of life only exists within our Conscious awareness to its Presence, the now. Any experience of the mind outside of a Conscious awareness of life is an unawareness or false awareness of life's existence. If one has no awareness to life's existence in the now, what is happening in the Present, there is a death experience within the mind.

One example of the mind's unconsciousness with no awareness to life in the now is when we see a person having no memory of life's occurrences during a specific time. For example, this can happen when driving home from work and later thinking that you don't even remember the drive itself. There is no memory of the drive home because you were not fully Present of mind to experience life's occurring in order to create a memory of it.

The false awareness or separate self-awareness is an illusion from the unconscious mind's death experience. It is the mind that separates itself from its Oneness with life, the environment, and others. In the creation of the separate self-awareness, a false self or ego identity emerges. As we see within the mind's positioning of separating itself from life's reality of the Present, the now, the ego is tempted by desires to seek more beyond life's only existence. The ego is never content with the here and now of life and is always searching for more or better than what it is already experiencing.

As the writer continues in Genesis, we see that Adam and Eve are now outside God's Presence (the Conscious awareness to life in the now), having hidden themselves from the existence of life (the mind's positioning of Being Present in the now). The ego, the false self-identity, leaves life's Present reality by its continual seeking for more than what is found in the now of Being One with life.

Through the mind's unawareness of life's Presence in the now of reality, the mind has fallen from its upright position of Consciousness to a lower level or false self-awareness. The ego identity separates the mind from God Consciousness or the awareness to life's Presence in the now. The ego or false self is an illusion to the only reality of life.

Sin—The Falling Away

The Bible's reference to *sin*—a Greek term for "missing the mark"—is another word to describe the *falling away from God's Presence* that we are introduced to in the allegory. The Bible refers to *the human sin nature*, for we have fallen away from God's Presence, Being One with life. It is through our mind's positioning that we have missed the mark of its right standing (righteousness), or it has fallen from a Conscious awareness to life's reality found in the now to a lower positioning, the unawareness of life's true existence. We are *dead in our sins* as the Bible says, for we have positioned our minds to an unawareness of life's Presence and are now experiencing a death within. We are *deprived of life* when we have fallen away from Presence, for we have left life's only reality of existence.

In our falling away from Being Present in this moment of reality, we have *fallen* from the mind's upright position; we have fallen from the mind's higher place of existence, our true identity of Being One with the Presence of life, One with our awareness of God.

Led Astray by a False Identity

The mind that has fallen from its Present awareness of life occurring in the now chooses to seek for more than what is. It looks for life beyond the very existence of its reality. In its seeking for more than what is occurring, it resists life, the alignment with its true identity. The mind has fallen from its true Oneness and identity to life, to a separateness of life, a false identity. The Bible refers to this false identity as things of the *flesh* or *pride*, for *God hates pride*. We should humble ourselves, lose the pride, this false self-identity, and come back to His Presence, that is, the Presence of life in the here and now of reality.

The mind that has strayed from its true identity, merging into separateness from the existence of life itself, develops this false identity of who it truly is. It leaves its right position, its righteousness, its alignment with life, its true identity. The falling away creates a separate identity for the mind, a separate self from the Oneness of life. The mind now becomes self-righteous, creating an ego identity, a self-image. The ego, the false self-identity, has fallen away from the Present awareness of life's now occurring. The mind, in its seeking for more than what is, has fallen from Presence to an unreality, a nonexistence of life. The ego, the false self-identity, does not live in the light of awareness to life in the Present moment. The false self resists life in its continual seeking for more, its impulsive desires having discontentment with what is. The longer the mind has fallen from Presence, a Present state of mind, the more it manifests the false image, the ego state. The more the mind separates itself from the reality of life, the deeper the mind sinks into an unreality, a death experience of life. The death experience creates darkness, hopelessness, a mental torment, for the mind has left the reality of life in its resistance to its Presence.

The ego or false self denies its awareness to the Presence of life in the now. It is an *enemy* to manifesting the image of life in the Present moment. The Bible refers to the enemy of God as the mind's position of doing its *own* will. The false self, being separated from its awareness of the natural flow of life in the Present moment, has taken on its own self-will, its own intentions and ability to do things. It has left the Present moment's natural flow of life's existence to seek its own path. The ego mind resists life, its natural path and flow of the unfolding of itself, as it is. It looks for a separate path outside of the flow of life, a path that will always be in resistance to reality. This will always result in hardship and strife. The mind's torment that lies outside life's Presence.

$\mathcal{T}$HE MIND IS A BATTLEFIELD

The war within is between the kingdom of light and the kingdom of darkness. The battle is between the existence of life, in your awareness to its Presence, and your unawareness to life's reality. Come into the light of awareness of My Presence within you! Come find Me, life in the Present moment, the existence of My Kingdom. For if you leave My Presence, your awareness of it, then you have become darkened within your mind because you are no longer aware of life. You have entered death in your mind's absence to life!

The darkened mind is not aware of life in the Present moment. It has left Conscious awareness to an unconscious state of mind—it is not aware of life found only in the now of Being One with it.

The Kingdom of Light and the Kingdom of Darkness

The Kingdom of God, life's existing Presence within you, is revealed through your Conscious awareness of it. You become aware of the existence of life that is flowing through you. In the light of your awareness to life, you are completely Conscious of your breath, your aliveness, and the existence of your Being. You have fully trusted and surrendered to life in the moment. You are aware of the flow of life within you and all around you. You are One with life in the Present moment, not separate to its existence, for it sustains you. Without the energy life force, you would not be alive. When you come to the awareness of your Being, its aliveness, you have surrendered to a Present awareness of the Kingdom of God, the energy flow of life that is within you! In your awareness, you have entered into a moment of Consciousness, fully aware of Being alive in the now. No life exists beyond a Conscious awareness of it.

Your victory or your defeat is within your awareness to the reality of life. For the mind is the battlefield; life is found in the now, in the Present.

The mind's experiences of past and future are a certain death to the reality of life's existence. Surrender to the light of a Conscious awareness of life in the now!

$\mathcal{J}$UDGMENT—THE DARKENED MIND

Oh, I have tasted the darkness, the judgment, and the condemnation bestowed upon me! I have felt the very back of God turned against me, but it was I who looked away from Him! I have felt the mental torment and anguish, guilt and shame. I have felt the deepest, darkest pit rise up all around me. My mind was left to soak in its murky waters. Without the light of awareness, I sank deeper and deeper into the thoughts that consumed my mind. I was without the awareness of life itself, the Presence of God. I cried out in anguish, for I had had enough! Take me from this mental slavery, dear Lord. Rescue me from the depths of condemnation! I cannot see my way out, and darkness surrounds me! *Jesus,* I cried, *save me!* And out of the very mental pit in which I lay, arose a voice of authority! The light shone in my mind, I became immediately aware of the life that is within me, and the darkness folded. I am back in the awareness of Presence! I am back to the Conscious awareness of life within me and all around me! Peace has surrounded me, for I do not resist this moment of awareness to life within! Oh Divine light of Consciousness, I have been called by You! I am aware of Your saving Presence within me!

Arise, child; you have been called out of the darkness and into the light of awareness! You have been set free from your mind, its torment of death!

ℱEAR

All fear takes root in the unconscious mind, its conditioned thinking, which has led you away from your awareness of life's reality in the Present moment. For it is in the absence of our awareness to life that we have shifted our mind's positioning into an unconsciousness state. We have left the reality of life in that moment.

To remain in Presence, we must surrender to it, fully trusting and believing in the now of life, its existence and flow.

𝒜FFLICTION

Your affliction shall be wiped away in the light of My Presence! Let not fear be troublesome to you. Instead, be aware of My grace, My flow of energy that is within you. For everyone who enters into the awareness of My Presence shall find mercy at My hand. Fear not, for your troubles are momentary. The mental torment shall not last long if you choose to seek Me out! I shall vindicate you. I shall lift you up in times of affliction and I shall carry you through this storm that rages within! Come, be enlightened to My ever-Present existence within you!

𝒯HE GOD OF BREAKTHROUGH

The light of awareness shines upon the darkened mind to reveal what is hidden; the light reveals the magnificent Being of life itself. Yet you have taken your awareness of this Present moment of life and hidden it. Come back into Conscious awareness of the life that exists in you! Come out of the darkness of your mind through the light of awareness of life!

As you fumble within the darkened mind, seeking a way out, you look for the light of awareness to shine through. Then you ask, When will this light pierce through my darkness and reveal to me the hope I long for? When will the light appear? Oh light, why have You forsaken me so? When will You pierce my awareness and free me from my despair? Then you think, I shall call out to my God of salvation, the Great God of breakthrough! The God of life will shine the light of awareness piercing through this darkness and save me.

Oh, God of life, shine the light of awareness upon me! Bring me to Your Presence, the awareness of Your existence within me! And then I shall no longer sink into the pit of despair! I shall call upon the Great God of breakthrough, and in this Present moment of awareness, I am brought out of the darkness and into Your glorious Presence!

A few will choose the path to life, this Present moment existence. Who desires to give up the seeking mind of all earthly things? Who has surrendered their heart's desires of seeking worldly pleasures and material possessions? In the seeking for more, he has left the very Presence of Being One with life in the now. Yet he who conquers the self, the ego's seeking for more, overcomes the desires of this world, and then he shall inherit the light of life, his awareness to its unfolding Presence!

ℱALSE TEACHINGS OF THE WORLD

The world will teach you from birth to death that you are a separate identity, a separate individual, a distinct self. That is, you are a seeker conditioned by the world to attain more and to be more in order to be fulfilled. The self must protect its self-interests; it must defend itself, to be above everyone else, in order to exist. The ego continues to search the world in self-seeking, to make itself whole and complete. The self continues to resist the Present moment because it is continually seeking for more outside of what is. The self-seeking mind-set is never at peace; it never rests. It is always in a continual focus on *more* and is never content with what is. The ego, the false self you have created, leads you away from the reality of life. The reality of life is only found in the Present moment. In Presence, you are One with just Being. You are one with life itself. You defy the reality of life when you continue to mentally seek outside of living in the Present moment.

Your thoughts and desires have led you astray from the reality of living life in the now. God is Presence; He is found in the Present moment. God is life, found only in the Present moment of simply Being One with it. You become One with God, One with life, One with Being, One with all there is, when you surrender your seeking mind to a stillness of what is.

The things of the world have deceived you, leading you astray from Me. You are never satisfied with what is in this moment. You continue to seek for more than Being One with life and its unfolding Presence!

I strayed away from the awareness of His Presence too far and for too long. And that was my suffering.

ℒET NOT YOUR MIND BE DECEIVED

Let not your mind be deceived by false truths, by a reality that does not exist! By not allowing your mind to surrender to My Presence, this Present moment awareness of life, you have entered an unreality. For no life exists beyond My Spirit; no life exists beyond the Present moment! Come back My Presence; become Consciously aware of what is! Let not your mind lead you astray from the only Presence of life that exists!

The self you have created is My enemy. It is in defiance of Me, and it resists your awareness of Being One with Me. Do not alienate your heart from Me, for your thinking will become futile, and darkness shall overtake you.

𝒴OUR FALSE SELF-IMAGE

You are not the self, the ego, as you imagined your identity to be. The self within you is a false representation of what is; a counterfeit of life. The ego is a manifestation of self-image, resisting what is, in search for its own separate identity. The ego manifests pride and a sense of higher worth or importance. The ego, the false self, resists the Presence of simply Being. The false self-identity always continues to seek outside the Present moment in search of more to add to its worth. It refuses to surrender to what is Present, to become One with the true reality of life, to become One with just Being.

We know that we are made in God's image, and not the false self-image. The ego is not who we are; it is not a reality of what is. Rather, we are the manifestation of God in Being One with life, One with what is, One with the Present moment. The ego always leads your mind away from life, from an alignment with life's Presence.

Remain humble, surrendering the ego to allow Conscious awareness to rise within your mind to a Present state of Being. That is all there is: life in the now. You are God, the life force expressing itself through your human form.

Trust what is, surrendering the false self. Let go, and allow Presence to overtake you! The ego seeks the world and all things in it, resisting the Presence of Being. The selfless surrender to what is, the Presence of Being One with life, the only reality!

$\mathcal{D}$ECEPTION

It is the ego that deceives you of life! The false self leads you astray from My manifestation within you. The ego is not satisfied with Being One with life, so it deceives you to leave Me in search for more. But I tell you, there is no more beyond Me, beyond the reality of life. Life is only found in the Present moment! Surrender to what is, to My Presence, to life. Your mind will deceive you to think of the past or seek the future that is outside of life, this Present moment. In the deception of your mind, you have left reality and missed life in that moment!

Remain in life, in the awareness of it in the Present moment, so that you may have life in you!

The truth will set you free! The truth of God's manifestation within you, your true identity, will set the ego, the false self, free! The truth of who you really are and why you were created frees the ego, the pride, and the false self-identity inside.

𝒯HE METAPHORICAL *TREE OF KNOWLEDGE OF GOOD AND EVIL*, FOUND WITHIN *THE GARDEN*, IS THE DESIRE TO KNOW WHAT LIES BEYOND OR EXISTS OUTSIDE OF A CONSCIOUS AWARNESS TO LIFE'S PRESENCE.

And out of the ground made the L<small>ORD</small> *God to grow every tree that is pleasant to the sight, and good for food; the tree of life **also in the midst of the garden**, and **the tree of knowledge of good and evil**. (Genesis 2:9 KJV)*

𝒯HE MIND'S EXPERIENCE OF LIVING THROUGH A CONSCIOUS AWARENESS OF LIFE IN THE PRESENT MOMENT; AND THE MIND'S EXPERIENCE OF EXISTING IN AN UNCONSCIOUS STATE, AN UNAWARENESS TO LIFE'S PRESENCE, OR DEATH.

And the L<small>ORD</small> *God commanded the man, saying, "You may surely eat of every tree of the garden, **but of the tree of the knowledge of good and evil you shall not eat**, for in the day that you eat of it you shall surely die." (Genesis 2:16–17 KJV)*

𝒴OUR MIND IS DECEIVED BY THE DESIRE TO SEEK MORE THAN WHAT LIES BEYOND LIFE'S ONLY EXISTENCE, THE PRESENT MOMENT.

*But the serpent said to the woman, "You will not surely die. For God knows that when you eat of it your eyes will be opened, and you will be like God, knowing good and evil." So when the woman saw that the tree was good for food, and that it was **a delight to the eyes**, and that the tree **was to be desired** to make one wise, she took of its fruit and ate, and she also gave some to her husband who was with her, and he ate. (Genesis 3:4–6 KJV)*

$\mathscr{A}$ FALSE SELF-AWARENESS OR FALSE SELF-IDENTITY IS CREATED WITHIN THE MIND WHEN IT IS SEPARATED FROM THE REALITY OF LIFE'S PRESENCE.

Then the eyes of both were opened, and they knew that they were naked. *(Genesis 3:7 KJV)*

$\mathscr{T}$HE MIND'S FALL FROM A PRESENT STATE, GOD CONSCIOUSNESS, TO A LOWER LEVEL – ONE OF A FALSE SELF-AWARENESS. A FALSE IDENTITY IS CREATED WITHIN THE MIND WHEN IT IS SEPARATED FROM LIFE'S ONLY REALITY.

The Fall

And they heard the sound of the LORD *God walking in the garden in the cool of the day, and **the man and his wife hid themselves from the presence of the** LORD **God** among the trees of the garden. (Genesis 3:8 KJV)*

$\mathscr{T}$HE MIND'S POSITIONING OF AN UNAWARENESS TO LIFE'S PRESENCE IN THE NOW, IS A DEATHLIKE EXPERIENCE. LIFE IS OCCURRING AND STILL EXISTING, BUT YOU ARE NOT PRESENT OF MIND TO WITNESS IT.

But the LORD ***God called*** *to the man and said to him, "**Where are you?**" And he said, "I heard the sound of you in the garden, **and I was afraid**, because I was naked, and **I hid myself**." (Genesis 3:9–10 KJV)*

$\mathscr{T}$HE MIND HAS SOUGHT AN EXPERIENCE BEYOND LIFE'S ONLY EXISTENCE, THE PRESENT MOMENT. YOUR MIND HAS BEEN SENT OUT OF LIFE'S EXISTENCE IN ITS SEEKING BEYOND THE REALITY OF ITS PRESENCE.

Therefore the Lord **God sent him out from the garden** *of Eden to work the ground from which he was taken.* **He drove out the man***, and at the east of the garden of Eden he placed the cherubim and a flaming sword that turned every way* **to guard the way to the tree of life***. (Genesis 3:23–24 KJV)*

$\mathcal{T}$HE MIND IS THE BATTLEFIELD—THE KINGDOM OF THE LIGHT OF AWARENESS AND THE KINGDOM OF DARKNESS (THE MIND'S UNAWARENESS TO LIFE IN THE NOW).

For we do not wrestle against flesh and blood, but against *the rulers, against the authorities, against the cosmic powers over* **this present darkness, against the spiritual forces of evil in the heavenly places***. (Ephesians 6:12)*

$\mathcal{T}$HE EYE (PINEAL) IS THE MIND'S CONCSIOUS AWARENESS (LAMP) TO LIFE IN THE NOW. A HEALTHY STATE OF MIND IS ONE THAT IS FULL OF THE LIGHT OF AWARENESS TO LIFE'S PRESENCE NOW OCCURRING. WITHOUT THE LIGHT OF AWARENESS OF LIFE'S PRESENCE, YOU ARE EXISTING IN THE DARKENED MIND.

*"***The eye*** is the lamp of the body. So,* **if your eye is healthy***, your whole body will be full of light, but* **if your eye is bad***,* **your whole body will be full of darkness***. If then the light in you is darkness, how great is the darkness! (Matthew 6:22–23)*

> *For* **with you is the fountain of life***;*
> **in your light do we see light***. (Psalm 36:9)*

This is the message we have heard from him and proclaim to you, that **God is light, and in him is no darkness at all***. (1 John 1:5)*

But you are a chosen race, a royal priesthood, a holy nation, a people for his own possession, that you may proclaim the excellencies of **him who called you out of darkness into his marvelous light**. *(1 Peter 2:9)*

But if anyone walks in the night, *he stumbles, because* **the light is not in him**. *(John 11:10)*

To open their eyes, *so that they may* **turn from darkness to light** *and from the power of Satan to God, that they may receive forgiveness of sins and a place among those who are sanctified by faith in me. (Acts 26:18)*

> **To give light to those who sit in darkness** *and* **in the shadow of death**,
>> *to guide our feet into the way of peace.*
>> *(Luke 1:79)*

Again Jesus spoke to them, saying, "**I am the light of the world**. *Whoever follows me will* **not walk in darkness, but will have the light of life**." *(John 8:12)*

For at **one time you were darkness**, *but* **now you are light in the Lord**. *Walk as children of light. (Ephesians 5:8)*

For God, who said, "**Let light shine out of darkness**," **has shone in our hearts** *to give* **the light of the knowledge of the glory of God in the face of Jesus Christ**. *(2 Corinthians 4:6)*

> *The* **people dwelling in darkness have seen a great light**,
>> *and for those dwelling in the region and shadow of death,*
>> **on them a light has dawned**. *(Matthew 4:16)*

> *For it is you who* **light** *my lamp;*
>> **the Lord my God lightens my darkness**.
>> *(Psalm 18:28)*

> Arise, shine, **for your light has come,**
>> and **the glory of the Lord has risen upon you.**
>> *(Isaiah 60:1)*

$\mathcal{T}$HIS FALLING AWAY IS A *DEBASED* MIND. IT HAS FALLEN TO A LOWER STANDARD, A LOWER QUALITY OF VALUE, NOT HAVING THE AWARENESS TO LIFE IN THE PRESENT. THE MIND IS NOT UPRIGHT IN ITS RIGHT POSITIONING TO LIFE IN THE NOW.

And since they did not see fit to acknowledge God, God gave them up to **a debased mind** to do what ought not to be done. They were filled with all manner of **unrighteousness,** evil, covetousness, malice. *(Romans 1:28–29)*

$\mathcal{P}$**RIDE** AND THINGS OF THE *FLESH* ARE BIBLICAL REFERENCES TO THE FALSE SELF-AWARENESS. THE EGO IDENTITY HAS BEEN CREATED WITHIN THE MIND AS IT SEPARATES FROM LIFE'S PRESENCE IN THE NOW.

> **The pride of your heart has deceived you,**
>> *you who live in the clefts of the rock,*
>> in **your lofty dwelling,**
> who say in your heart,
>> "**Who will bring me down** to the ground?"
>> *(Obadiah 1:3)*

For if anyone thinks he is something, when he is nothing, **he deceives himself.** *(Galatians 6:3)*

Let no one deceive himself. If anyone among you thinks that he is wise in this age, let him become a fool that he may become wise. *(1 Corinthians 3:18)*

But for those who are self-seeking and do not obey the truth, but obey **unrighteousness,** there will be wrath and fury. *(Romans 2:8)*

> *For the sin of their mouths,*
> *the words of their lips,*
> **let them be trapped in their pride**. *(Psalm 59:12)*

*For people will be **lovers of self**, lovers of money, **proud**, **arrogant**, abusive, disobedient to their parents, ungrateful, **unholy** …. (2 Timothy 3:2)*

*C*HE FALSE SELF OR EGO IDENTITY RESISTS LIVING IN A PRESENT STATE OF MIND; IT SEEKS FOR MORE BEYOND THE PRESENT BECAUSE IT IS NOT SATISFIED WITH WHAT IS IN THE NOW OCCURRING.

*Keep your life **free from love of money**, and **be content with what you have**, for he has said, "**I will never leave you nor forsake you**." (Hebrews 13:5)*

*He must not be a recent convert, or he may **become puffed up with conceit and fall** into the condemnation of the devil. (1 Timothy 3:6)*

*Treacherous, reckless, **swollen with conceit**, **lovers of pleasure rather than lovers of God** …. (2 Timothy 3:4)*

> **Be not wise in your own eyes**;
> **fear the Lord,** and turn away from evil.
> (Proverbs 3:7)

*For **they all seek their own interests**, not those of Jesus Christ. (Philippians 2:21)*

Do not love the world or the things in the world. If anyone loves the world, the love of the Father is not in him. For all that is in the world—the desires of the flesh and the desires of the eyes and pride of life—is not from the Father but is from the world. *(1 John 2:15–16)*

*We know that we are from God, and **the whole world lies in the power of the evil one**. (1 John 5:19)*

*And that they will come to their senses **and escape from the trap of the devil, who has taken them captive to do his will.** (2 Timothy 2:26 NIV)*

*In their case **the god of this world has blinded the minds of the unbelievers**, to keep them from seeing the light of the gospel of the glory of Christ, **who is the image of God**. (2 Corinthians 4:4)*

*You adulterous people! Do you not know that **friendship with the world is enmity with God**? **Therefore whoever wishes to be a friend of the world makes himself an enemy of God**. (James 4:4)*

*For the **one who sows to his own flesh will from the flesh reap corruption**, but the **one who sows to the Spirit will from the Spirit reap eternal life**. (Galatians 6:8)*

> *But if you will not listen,*
> *   **my soul will weep in secret for your pride**;*
> *my eyes will weep bitterly and run down with tears,*
> *   **because the L<small>ORD</small>'s flock has been taken captive**. (Jeremiah 13:17)*

*For the wages of **sin is death**, but the **free gift of God is eternal life in Christ Jesus** our Lord. (Romans 6:23)*

*For **those who live according to the flesh set their minds on the things of the flesh**, but **those who live according to the Spirit set their minds on the things of the Spirit. For to set the mind on the flesh is death, but to set the mind on the Spirit is life and peace**. (Romans 8:5–6)*

***Forsaking the right way, they have gone astray**. (2 Peter 2:15)*

> *We all, like sheep, **have gone astray**,*
>   ***each of us has turned to our own way*** ….
>   *(Isaiah 53:6 NIV)*

But each person is tempted when he is lured and enticed by his own desire. *Then desire when it has conceived gives birth to sin, and **sin when it is fully grown brings forth death**. (James 1:14–15)*

Chapter 2.5

The Need for a Savior—The Death of Our False Self-Identity

In the light of our Conscious awareness to life's existing in the now, we know the truth of who we are, our true identity, our Oneness with life itself in the Presence of it. In the fullness of the alert and awake mind, we are Present and One with life, its life flow energy that sustains us in this moment. This is our mind's right-standing position, having come into an alignment with life's Presence in the here and now of reality. We are the manifestation of life in its unfolding of itself in and through us. We are One with Spirit, One with God's manifestation that is gifting us with our Being and aliveness in this moment. We are the Conscious awareness within that is experiencing the world and all things in it.

Now, in our mind's temptation, our desire to know more or to seek more beyond life's reality, we have stepped out of the Present state of awareness in our search for more than what is. We have stepped outside life's Presence, the reality of its existence in the now occurring, to an unreality, a pseudo-life, an illusion or death, to what is. In our separation from our awareness to life's Presence, we have created a false self-awareness. Our true identity, our mind's position of right standing, has now fallen to a lower level of unawareness, a false reality, a false self-identity. Our mind's positioning has been led astray from the Presence of life's reality by the ego, which is the false self that is seeking outside of the here and now for more than what is naturally occurring.

The Need for a Savior

We now exist outside the Presence of life; our mind's awareness to life's existence has now fallen to a level of unawareness to life's only reality. In our self-awareness we have separated the mind from the awareness of life itself. We have assumed a false identity that leads us away from life's existence. We have no awareness to life in the Present moment, and we are now in need of a savior. We are in need of someone who will show us the way back to our true identity, our Oneness with life itself, in the Present moment of its existence. We are in need of someone who will show us that this false self-awareness, this ego identity, which is in search of more, something beyond life's reality, is not our true identity. We have been deceived and robbed of life that is found only in the Present moment. We need to be led back to the light of the awareness of life, and back to the truth of *who* we are. *But how would we know the way ….?*

In the light of Conscious awareness to life's Presence, you will know the truth of who you are. No one comes to the Father, the awareness of life that is found in the Present moment, except through Me, the death of your false self.

The Way

The greatest teacher proclaiming the Kingdom of God, His knowledge of God's abiding Presence, and His teachings on how to enter into this Eternal life of existence, was Jesus. He was the *Christ,* the *Messiah*, the promised *savior* of the world who would deliver us from our fall from Being One with God. Jesus said He was the *light of the world*, having the light of Conscious awareness in Him. He said *He was God, One with Eternal life* itself. Jesus knew His mind's right-standing position, being Consciously aware, present in mind, living in the Present moment of reality, which is Eternal life. Jesus knew His identity, becoming One with life in the Presence of it—One with God. Jesus said, *I and the Father are One*. I and the life flow energy that allows for my existence of Being, that is *God*, are One. Jesus remained in alignment with His true identity, His union and Oneness with life's Presence (God), through living in the Present moment of a Conscious awareness to life itself.

Jesus was God, and as He said, we too are all gods; that is, in our belief or light of awareness to life's existence in the

Present moment, we become One with life itself. Yet we have fallen from our awareness of life in the Present and created a false self-awareness and an ego identity that leads us away from life's Presence to seek more than what is. How could Jesus show us the way back into our mind's awareness of life's Presence, back into our Oneness with it, living in the Present moment of existence? How could we shake this false self-identity, this ego that is always in search for more than what is, and get back to our true nature, our true identity and Oneness with life itself? Jesus said He was going to go and prepare a place for us and come back to get us, so that we could again dwell in the Presence of life. Jesus said *He was the way* that would lead us back to living in the Presence of life, One with God, our true identity.

The Way Back to Life's Presence Is a Death of the False Self-Awareness

Jesus, being One with God, One with life in the full Presence of its existence, fulfilled His calling, His life's purpose. As we see right before His capture and arrest, Jesus died to His self-will to allow the purpose of life to be carried out. We also see that He surrendered all temptation that the enemy (ego) attempted to deceive Him with in the desert. For we know Jesus was offered all the riches of life, all the impulsive desires, if He would step outside of Life's purpose, outside of life's reality to attain them.

Jesus taught us that if we trusted life's existence (believed in God), the reality of its only Presence found in the Present moment, its natural unfolding of itself, we would come back to the light of Conscious awareness. We would no longer believe in our false self-awareness but in life itself, its very Presence of existence within us. If we too deny our false self-will, the desire to seek life beyond its only existence of the Present moment, we too will become One with life again. As we know, Jesus accepted the call of life, His purpose, and God's plan, to show us all that if we die to false self-awareness, we not only experience Eternal life while we are still living here but will continue to exist in a Oneness with life even when we leave our mortal bodies. As we know, Jesus was crucified on the cross and resurrected, fully restored to life again three days later. Jesus showed us that if we remain in a Present state of mind through a Conscious awareness of our Oneness with life in the now, we shall never die (the mind's death like experience) for we are now living in the Presence of life's existence. It is through our surrender of the false self-will, and putting to death our ego that we too will find our way back to the Present moment of life's reality. Jesus said we must deny ourselves daily, take up our cross, and follow Him. We deny the false self and die to the ego's seeking for more, and then we too know our way back to our true selves, our Oneness with life. When we die to our false self, fully surrendering to life as it is occurring, we have a mind that is fully Present, awake and aware of life's existence in the now. To come back with Jesus and dwell in the Presence of life, this *preparing of the way* of which He spoke, is the death of our ego, the false-self awareness that we created within the mind. To surrender the false self-identity, letting go of seeking more beyond this Present moment of life's only reality, is to come back fully restored to our Oneness with life, with God, in the now occurring.

It is the ego that holds you captive to do its will. It holds your mind in bondage, keeping you away from the present moment of life, the true reality of life. But it is through the death of the ego's seeking mind that you come back to your awareness of Me! You come back to life! You have denied your self-awareness and have come back to the Oneness of life in the now! Your death has prepared a place for your dwelling within Me!

The veil of deceit is your false self-identity! It has blinded you from seeing life in the Present moment. When the veil has been removed, in the death of the self, the Glory of God is manifested in you! You are One with life in the Present moment of your awareness to it! You are One with the very nature of life, One with God.

$\mathcal{T}$HE TWO DEATHS WE WILL EXPERIENCE—THE SYMBOLIC PURPOSE OF THE CROSS

How much trust You had, Jesus, when You were alone with the Father, and He revealed to You His plan for Your life! Oh! How faithful You must have been to the Father when all was revealed, that You would be betrayed, beaten, and crucified! And You trusted Him! To the point of death, You remained fully surrendered to allow His Presence, life's unfolding of itself, to manifest through You. You spent much time seeking the Father in desolate places, the desert and the mountains, in solitude, away from the world's distractions. For we know, just as we are tempted by the false self, the ego's seeking for more, You too were tempted in the wilderness. You were offered the world and all it had to offer, if You had chosen to follow the ego's desires. Yet You overcame the world and chose to live without seeking for more than what was handed to You. You surrendered to life's Presence in its unfolding of itself. You gave up all that the world had to offer You, and You died upon the cross instead. You overcame the world to gain the light of life, Your Conscious awareness of it, in the now of its Presence of existence. And through the natural unfolding of life, in Your surrender to His purpose for You, what He wanted to do through You was completed. In our surrender of seeking more than what is, we all shall overcome the world just as You did so that we might surrender to life as it is, in Being One with Presence! We all shall overcome our selves, and the world's enticements, its lure of a false reality, and die with You! We are those who wish to remain in God, in the Present moment of life's existence, and to allow His will, life's unfolding of itself, to be done. For that, we shall all die a continual death. And upon our death, we have surrendered to life's only reality in the Present moment, in the now of Being fully Conscious to all there is!

Keep your mind fully Present, aware of this moment, and the false self will cease to exist!

Born Again

Now that you have died to your false-self awareness, the ego's seeking for more outside of life's Presence, you must be *born again* to enter the Kingdom of God, as Jesus claimed. Having been born again into the light of awareness to life's Presence, a mind has become awakened to its Oneness with life again. Our minds have been born into God Consciousness, our true identity, for we have surrendered the false self. We have been born again through a mind that has come to a Present state of awareness to life in the now.

Jesus said after we have denied ourselves, then we are to believe (in God, Spirit, the life flow energy within) and be baptized (the immersing into the light of awareness). We are *born again* in the light of awareness, our belief in life (Spirit), its natural flow of energy that is sustaining us in this moment.

We are now *baptized*, having our minds fully immersed into our light of Conscious awareness of life's only Presence. We are again One with Spirit, One with the awareness of life. Our minds are fully awake and Conscious of life's unfolding. We are One with life, its natural occurring, in our awareness of it. We are now in our minds' right-standing position, our righteousness, having aligned ourselves or come into the agreement of life's Presence. We have been born again into the light of awareness of Being Present to our aliveness, to our breath, to the Spirit of God manifesting within us. We now see that we are a new creation, a new identity; we are God's manifestation. We have been born again.

There must be a death in order for there to be a rebirth! You must be born again into the Conscious awareness of becoming One with life, One with Being. Put to death your false self-identity, this false-self awareness you have created, and be reborn into the awareness of life's Presence, the only reality of life's existence.

Resurrected and Fully Restored to Life

Jesus surrendered His self-will in order to carry out God's calling and plan for His life. We are shown that it is through our surrendered false-self awareness that we align with our true identity, our Oneness with God, our Oneness with life's Presence of reality. In our denial or death of the ego, we are fully resurrected, having our minds restored to their right-standing position, immersed into the light of awareness of life in the Presence of it. We are fully surrendered to life in the now occurring, its natural flow. We are One with life, no longer in resistance to it, for we have surrendered to this moment. Jesus remained in the light, the light of awareness to life in the Present, and although He died a physical death, He was resurrected, fully restored to life. He remained in Eternal life's Presence, this now of everlasting existence.

The more you seek of this world, the less you will have of Me.

$\mathcal{T}$HE CHRIST, THE ANOINTING OF LIFE

The Christ, the anointing of life, is the death of your self-awareness, your ego, to gain the mind's Conscious awareness of God's Presence within. Anointing of the Spirit is the mind's awareness of the breath, the life force energy that sustains you in this moment. You have surrendered the false-self awareness and have become awakened or anointed with life's Presence within you and all around you. You have lifted your head above your limited view of a separate self-identity and become aware to all that exists around you. You have emancipated yourself from the thinking and reasoning mind, the intellect, to a mind that is simply content in Being One with life through its awareness of it.

As Christ declared, you shall know the truth, and the truth shall set you free. The anointing of Spirit is freedom from the mind's searching of more than what is found in the Present moment of life. It is freedom from the ego's dissatisfaction of life in the here and now of Being One with it. This searching for more takes you away from God's Presence, a Present state of Being, Oneness with life in the now. When you surrender the ego, you surrender to Presence. Through the Present state of mind, you become Consciously aware of what is real, the truth of the only existence of life found in Being Present with it. This freedom of mind releases you from the ego's false awareness or false reality that seeks for life beyond its Presence.

Christ is the division, for the death of your self allows God's Being to emerge within you!

$\mathcal{W}$E ARE MADE TO OVERCOME

Has my mind deceived me? Has it led me from living in the Present moment, resisting life as it is? Surely it has! My thoughts continue to seek all that I don't have in this moment. My mind is restless, for it is resisting life in the now. I allow the thoughts to overcome my mind, seeking all that I don't have and the desire to have. And in all my thinking and seeking I have left life, found only in the Presence of it. Yes, I have left Being One with life because I am no longer content. My ego is not satisfied with what is in the now, so it deprives me of life, and it leads my mind astray in its seeking for more. Surely it has robbed me of life! It has distracted my awareness from Being Present in the now. It has led me from the only life there is, the true reality, to an unreality, a death.

As I look to this great revelation of who I am, the expression of life itself, I am in awe of how much I have been deceived and led astray from the awareness of it. How much of my existence has been spent in unreality, a falsification of life? How long have I existed in death, unconscious, unaware to life in the Presence of its existence? For I have no memory of life when my mind has left the now. I have been completely forgotten! I will overcome this false self, this ego that has imprisoned my mind and robbed me of life! I will die to its illusion. I will give it no more of my mind. Instead, I will fully surrender to my Conscious awareness of this Present moment, and I will become One with life, One with Being, One with reality. I will overcome this!

The manifestation of Presence within you requires total surrender of the self. Be awakened to life in your mind's full surrender to it!

ℒOOKING INTO THE MIRROR OF TRUTH

Our true alignment, who we really are, can only be realized once we have died to our false self, our ego. It is the awareness of our position, our right standing in God's Presence, to become One with Being. In the death of our egos, we have surrendered our false image and allowed the emergence of God's Presence within us.

ℐ HAVE FOUND LIFE

I can endure all perceived trials that my ego manifests because I am convinced that seeking shelter in a Present state of mind is the only life that does exist. My ego has created an illusion, an unreal representation of what is! It has deceived me of life, its fullness of what is this now of its existence. When I remain fully in the Present, becoming One with life, I am free from all the mental torment, the illusions of an unreality. I am free from any bondage, fully surrendered to the truth and reality of life's Presence. I am here in this moment, with all that exists, in the Presence of Being One with life.

ℛESURRECTION

It is the Christ, the anointing of life, that resurrects us. In our death, our minds have been delivered to the now of life's existence. Our light of awareness shows us we are not the false self, the ego manifestation. Rather, we are life's Presence manifesting within us. Our old life, our old way of self-seeking has surrendered to the Present moment, to what is. We have not resisted the reality of life through the seeking of more; rather, we have died to that way of thinking and embraced life in the Present. In our death, we are given resurrected life. We become aware of life, all that there is, found only in the Presence of Being One with it! Life, the true reality of what is, has been born within our awareness, for we know that nothing exists outside of the now, the Present moment of life's existence.

FREEING THE SELF

Freedom is letting go of the false self to a mental state nonresistant to the unfolding Presence of life. Freedom is surrendering and allowing life to exist as it is, simply Being in the Present moment. It is walking out life in the path of least resistance. There emerges an ease, a flow, an acceptance to what is.

In the absence of self, you will find Me, the existence of life.

TOTAL SURRENDER

Surrender to Me by freely letting go of your mind's seeking ways. There is nothing to seek outside the Present moment, for life only exists now. Do not resist life in this moment, but surrender to it, accepting it. Become fully alive in the Presence of life. I AM only found here! Life is only found in your surrender to it! Become One with just Being! I AM life, and I AM fully alive in you! Allow your mind to drift into a Conscious awareness of what is occurring in this very moment. Just for a moment, be content with what is. Truly, no life exists beyond what is in the now. Become One with the ease of life, the flow of life. Be mentally aware of Presence, Being Present with life in its unfolding of itself.

Unless one dies to the self, he continues to mentally step away from Being Present with life, forsaking its Presence. Let go of the self, and become self-less in the Kingdom of God!

I shall sacrifice my self, my false self-identity, to experience more moments of life as it is in the now, rather than perish in a death where life has no memory of me and I am completely forgotten.

Rise above the false self! For in your surrender you have victory! You have overcome the enemy, the false self, the pride, and the ego! Rise, child, and you shall surely be crowned in My Presence with the crown of life!

$\mathcal{T}$HE MIND'S FALL FROM THE LIGHT OF AWARENESS TO LIFE'S PRESENCE: THE NEED FOR A SAVIOR.

*For all have sinned **and fall** short **of the glory of God**. (Romans 3:23)*

Remember therefore from where you have fallen; repent, *and do the works you did at first. If not, I will come to you and* ***remove your lampstand*** *from its place, unless you repent. (Revelation 2:5)*

$\mathcal{T}$HE *LIVING* ARE THOSE WHO ARE CONSCIOUSLY AWARE OF LIFE'S PRESENCE IN THE NOW. THE LIVING KNOW *THEY DIE* (EGO OR THE FALSE SELF- AWARENESS) IN ORDER TO GAIN THE AWARENESS TO LIFE'S PRESENCE.

$\mathcal{T}$HE *DEAD* ARE THOSE WHO HAVE NO AWARENESS TO LIFE'S PRESENCE IN THE NOW. THE MIND CANNOT CREATE A MEMORY IF IT IS NOT PRESENT WITH LIFE IN THAT MOMENT.

For the living *know that* ***they will die***, *but* ***the dead know nothing***, *and they have no more reward, for* ***the memory of them is forgotten***. *(Ecclesiastes 9:5)*

$\mathcal{T}$HE WILL OR WAY OF THE FATHER (LIFE) IS TO BE PRESENT OR ONE WITH LIFE IN THE MOMENT; A PRESENT STATE OF MIND IS ENTERING INTO THE KINGDOM OF HEAVEN.

I Never Knew You

Not everyone who says to Me, "Lord, Lord," shall enter the kingdom of heaven, but he who does the will of My Father in heaven. *Many will say to Me in that day, "Lord, Lord, have we not prophesied in Your name, cast out demons in Your name,* and done many wonders in Your name?" And then I will declare to them, "**I never knew you**; depart from Me, you who practice lawlessness!" (Matthew 7:21–23)

$\mathcal{T}$HE WAY TO LIFE'S REALITY: TO DWELL IN PRESENCE (MY FATHER'S HOUSE). YOUR DEATH OF THE FALSE-SELF AWARENESS WILL PREPARE THE WAY TO A PRESENT STATE OF MIND.

In **my Father's house** are many **dwelling places**; if it were not so, I would have told you. I go to prepare a place for you.

And if I go and prepare a place for you, I will come again and take you unto myself; that where I am, there ye may be also.

So that ye know where I go, and ye know the way. (John 14:2–4)

$\mathcal{T}$HE *TRUTH* OR REALITY OF *LIFE* IS FOUND (THE *WAY*) IN THE MIND'S PRESENT STATE OF AWARENESS TO IT. TO COME TO THE FATHER (AN AWARENESS OF LIFE IN THE NOW) IS THROUGH THE MIND'S DEATH OF THE FALSE SELF-AWARENESS.

Thomas said to him, "Lord, we do not know where you are going. How can we know the way?" **Jesus said** to him, "**I am the way**, and **the truth**, and **the life**. **No one comes to the Father except through me**." (John 14:5–6)

$\mathcal{D}$EATH OF THE FALSE SELF

I have been crucified with Christ. It is **no longer I who live**, but **Christ who lives in me**. And the life I now live in the flesh I live by faith in the Son of God, who loved me and gave himself for me. (Galatians 2:20)

*Do you not know that all of us who have been baptized into Christ Jesus were **baptized into his death**?(Romans 6:3)*

*For Christ's love compels us, because we are convinced that one died for all, and **therefore all died**. (2 Corinthians 5:14 NIV)*

***We know that our old self was crucified with him** in order that the body of sin might be brought to nothing, so that we would no longer be enslaved to sin. (Romans 6:6)*

*For **you** have **died**, and **your life is hidden** with Christ in God. (Colossians 3:3)*

*And I heard a voice from heaven saying, "Write this: **Blessed are the dead who die in the Lord** from now on." "Blessed indeed," says the Spirit, "**that they may rest from their labors**, for their deeds follow them!" (Revelation 14:13)*

*Therefore **we have been buried with Him** through **baptism into death**, so that as Christ was raised from the dead through the glory of the Father, so we too might **walk in newness of life**. (Romans 6:4 NIV)*

*I protest, brothers, by my pride in you, which I have in Christ Jesus our Lord, **I die every day**! (1 Corinthians 15:31)*

As it is written,

> *"For your sake **we are being killed all the day long**;*
> *we are regarded as sheep to be slaughtered."*
> *(Romans 8:36)*

Take Up Your Cross

For whoever wishes to save his life will lose it**; but **whoever loses his life for My sake will find it**. For **what will it profit a man

if he gains the whole world and forfeits his soul? Or what will a man give in exchange for his soul? (Matthew 16:25–26 NASB)

Then Jesus said to his disciples, "Whoever wants to be my disciple must deny themselves and take up their cross and follow me." (Matthew 16:24 NIV)

But far be it from me to boast except in the cross of our Lord Jesus Christ, by which the world has been crucified to me, and I to the world. (Galatians 6:14)

He must increase, but I must decrease. (John 3:30)

$\mathcal{B}$ORN AGAIN—THE ANOINTING (BLESSING) OF SPIRIT: BEING IMMERSED INTO THE LIGHT OF AWARENESS OF THE REALITY OF LIFE FOUND IN A PRESENT STATE OF MIND.

Jesus answered him, "Truly, truly, I say to you, unless one is born again he cannot see the kingdom of God." (John 3:3)

Jesus answered, "Very truly I tell you, no one can enter the kingdom of God unless they are born of water and the Spirit. Flesh gives birth to flesh, but the Spirit gives birth to spirit. You should not be surprised at my saying, 'You must be born again.'" (John 3:5–7 NIV)

$\mathcal{T}$HE MIND OVERCOMES THE ILLUSION (THE WORLD THAT IS CREATED BY THE FALSE SELF-AWARENESS) WHEN IT COMES BACK TO A PRESENT STATE OF AWARENESS TO LIFE IN THE NOW.

For everyone who has been born of God overcomes the world. (1 John 5:4)

𝒜 MIND THAT IS BORN OF *SPIRIT* IS A MIND THAT IS PRESENT TO LIFE IN THE NOW OF REALITY. A MIND THAT IS BORN OF *FLESH* IS A MIND THAT IS CAUGHT UP IN THE ILLUSION OF THE FALSE SELF-AWARENESS (THE NON-REALITY OF LIFE).

That which is born of the flesh is flesh, and that which is born of the Spirit is spirit. (John 3:6)

𝓡ESURRECTED AND RESTORED TO THE PRESENCE OF LIFE.

*Jesus said to her, "***I am the resurrection and the life. Whoever believes in me, though he die, yet shall he live***, and ***everyone who lives and believes in me shall never die****. Do you believe this?" (John 11:25–26)*

*****For as in Adam all die, so also in Christ shall all be made alive****. (1 Corinthians 15:22)*

*For ***they cannot die anymore***, because they are equal to angels and are sons of God, ***being sons of the resurrection***. (Luke 20:36)*

𝒟*EATH* AND *HELL* IS THE STATE OF MIND THAT IS UNAWARE OF LIFE'S PRESENCE IN THE NOW OCCURING. THE MIND HAS LEFT A PRESENT STATE OF BEING ONE WITH IT THROUGH A FALSE SELF-AWARENESS OR NON-REALITY OF WHAT IS. *THE KEY* IS TO DIE TO THE EGO AND TO COME BACK TO LIFE'S PRESENCE IN THE HERE AND NOW.

*****I am the Living One; I was dead****, and now look, ***I am alive for ever*** and ever! And ***I hold the keys of death and Hades***. (Revelation 1:18 NIV)*

*Yet a little while and **the world will see me no more, but you will see me. Because I live, you also will live.** (John 14:19)*

***Be faithful unto death**, **and I will give you the crown of life**. (Revelation 2:10)*

Chapter 3

Inheriting the Kingdom— The Practice of Entering a Present State of Mind

Chapter 3.1

The Captive Thought: Your Weapon of Warfare

The Mind's Struggle for Life's Presence—The Spiritual Warfare

We know that the mind is the battlefield for inner psychological warfare. The mind's battle between its right positioning to the light of a Conscious awareness to life's Presence in the now occurring, and the fallen position of an unconscious unawareness of life's reality. The war is between the light of awareness of life in the now, and the darkened mind being unaware of life's now unfolding. It is the battle between life in its only existence of now, and a death experience, the stepping out of the reality of life's natural flow.

The ego, the false self-identity that we have created within our mind's separateness from life's now occurring, has led us astray to seek something beyond the Presence of life. This experience of an unreal "life" is an illusion, a counterfeit of life's only existence, the here and now. We have left a Present state of mind in its awareness to life's reality and have gone through a Spiritual death, the mind's unawareness to life's Presence.

The Captive Thought: Our Weapon in the Inner Psychological Warfare

As Jesus unfolded for us, we are to deny our false self-awareness, the ego's impulsive desiring and seeking for more outside the Presence of life. It is the ego that has enslaved our minds and deceived us to seek beyond Presence, the only reality of life. The ego holds our minds in bondage, existing outside the reality of life's Presence. The ego is a mind that is not content with what is but is driven by continual desires for more, never resting in the reality of life's Presence. The ego continually seeks for more than what exists. Our thoughts, being our driving force, lead us astray for more than what is, in the now. The ego denies the flow of life's naturally occurring path by stepping out of it to search and attain beyond life's reality. The ego chooses to deny life's Present moment and step out of it in search for its own self-interests, intentions, and desires. The ego or the unconscious mind has left the Present awareness of life's only existence.

Our weapon in the warfare of the life and death states is *holding each thought captive to Christ*—that is, denying its power by surrendering the seeking thoughts or allowing them to die within us. We have power to destroy the ego's stronghold by putting those thoughts to death. And when we have died to the mind's continual seeking because of its constant dissatisfaction, we have surrendered and aligned our minds to their right standing position of the here and now, life's true reality. We have come back into alignment with life's flow, the path of least resistance, our true identity Being One with life itself, One with God. Jesus was reminding us to remain in the Present moment when He said we should be content with what we have, for He (life's Presence) will never leave us (the Present Moment of life's existence).

Overcome the illusion of the false self-awareness, the darkened mind by becoming Present to life in the now.

Become Present of mind, and you shall gain life!

You are a prisoner of your mind's illusion until Christ sets you free!

$\mathcal{P}$**RISONER**

You are a prisoner held captive by your mind's seeking for more beyond My Presence. You are in bondage to your thoughts and desires. In your search for more, you have left Me, the reality of life. And in your search for more, you have created a separate identity from life, this ego or false self, which resists My Presence. It continues to seek and search, stepping out beyond Me, the true reality of life. Set those thoughts free, child, for they have held you in bondage, away from the only real existence of life. In your surrender, you have become One with Me again, this natural free flowing life force energy that is within and all around you.

Free your mind from its slavery, and come into this Present Moment awareness of life; come and experience the fullness of life in its now occurring.

You are no longer a slave to your self-seeking ways, for you have died to your-self! When you surrender to Presence, you are set free from the bondage that the ego creates!

$\mathcal{W}$HAT IS IT THAT YOU ARE SEEKING?

Have I not come to set the slaves free? Have I not come to break the chains of the oppressed? Have not your mind's focus, passion, and desires taken over you? Have you not been enslaved to such thinking? Have they not overtaken your mind to such an extent that you have been consumed with them, seeking them and chasing them down? This is futile. For in your continued mental seeking of what you did not have, you resisted life as it is! You resisted the Presence of Being One with life.

Surrender this seeking for more than what is, and come back to life's existence, this Present moment! It is a Conscious awareness of Being One with the flow of life, this here and now of reality.

You are not a slave to your mind's seeking anymore, for in the death of this seeking, you shall be set free to life's reality. Do not resist the awareness of this Present moment.

*E*XILE

The ego searches for more than what is now occurring; it is never satisfied with life's emerging Presence. The ego continues to seek outside the Present moment, resisting the joy of just Being One with life. When we resist what is, through our dissatisfaction with life, we stray from living in the Present moment. The ego mind continues to search for what it believes will make it whole and complete. Yet living in the Present moment is the whole of our Being, our Oneness to all there is. The ego will convince us that there is more, so it will leave a Present state of mind to seek out beyond what is. This mental walking away from what is, life in the moment, is an exile from Life's Presence. To come back to Presence, you must surrender to it—surrender the mental self-seeking of more and come to the acceptance of life found only in the Present moment.

$\mathcal{S}$PIRITUAL WARFARE IS THE BATTLE WITHIN THE MIND: THE MIND'S STRUGGLE WITHIN THE ILLUSION TO LIFE'S REALITY THROUGH ITS FALL FROM A PRESENT STATE OF MIND. THE MIND IS NOT PRESENT AND AWARE TO LIFE'S EXISTENCE IN THE NOW.

*For **we do not wrestle against flesh and blood**, but against the rulers, against the authorities, against the cosmic powers **over this present darkness, against the spiritual forces** of evil in the heavenly places. (Ephesians 6:12)*

$\mathcal{I}$MPULSIVE DESIRES OVERCOME YOU THROUGH TEMPTATION TO LEAVE A PRESENT STATE OF MIND AND ENTER INTO THE UNCONSCIOUS MIND; A STATE THAT IS NOT AWARE OF LIFE'S REALITY IN THE NOW.

*For **they mouth empty, boastful words** and, **by appealing to the lustful desires of the flesh**, they entice people who are just escaping from those who live in error. **They promise them freedom**, while they themselves are slaves of depravity—for **"people are slaves to whatever has mastered them." If they have escaped the corruption of the world** by knowing our Lord and Savior Jesus Christ **and are again entangled in it and are overcome,** they are worse off at the end than they were at the beginning. (2 Peter 2:18–20 NIV)*

*And they may come to their senses and escape from the snare of the devil, **after being captured by him to do his will**. (2 Timothy 2:26)*

> *The Spirit of the Lord G*od* is upon me,*
> *because the L*ord* has anointed me*
> *to bring good news to the poor;*
> *he has sent me to **bind up the brokenhearted,***
> ***to proclaim liberty to the captives**,*
> *and **the opening of the prison to those who***
> ***are bound** …. (Isaiah 61:1)*

In which he went and proclaimed to the spirits in prison ....
(1 Peter 3:19)

Since therefore the children share in flesh and blood, he himself likewise partook of the same things, **that through death he might destroy the one who has the power of death,** *that is, the devil, and* **deliver all those who through fear of death were subject to lifelong slavery.** *(Hebrews 2:14–15)*

> *To open the eyes that are blind,*
> **to bring out the prisoners from the dungeon,**
> > **from the prison those who sit in darkness.**
> > *(Isaiah 42:7)*

OUR WEAPON OF WARFARE IS HOLDING EACH THOUGHT CAPTIVE TO ITS DEATH (CHRIST).

Weapon of Warfare

For though we walk in the flesh, we are not waging war according to the flesh. **For the weapons of our warfare** *are not of the flesh but* **have divine power to destroy strongholds. We destroy arguments and every lofty opinion** *raised* **against the knowledge of God,** *and* **take every thought captive to obey Christ.** *(2 Corinthians 10:3–5)*

IN THE SURRENDERING OR DEATH OF THE THOUGHTS THAT SEEK BEYOND THE NOW, WE ARE AGAIN SET FREE FROM THE BONDAGE OF DEATH; THAT WHICH LIES BEYOND LIFE IN THE NOW OF ITS REALITY.

> **He brought them out of darkness** *and* **the shadow of death,**
> > *and* **burst their bonds apart.** *(Psalm 107:14)*

*But now we are released from the law, **having died to that which held us captive**, so that **we serve in the new way of the Spirit** and not in the old way of the written code. (Romans 7:6)*

*For **freedom Christ has set us free**; **stand firm** therefore, and **do not submit again to** a yoke of **slavery**. (Galatians 5:1)*

*Now the Lord is the Spirit**, and **where the Spirit of the Lord is**, **there is freedom**. (2 Corinthians 3:17)*

> *Who executes justice for the oppressed,*
> *who gives food to the hungry.*
> **The L**ord **sets the prisoners free** *…. (Psalm 146:7)*

Life in the Spirit

*There is therefore now no condemnation **for those who are in Christ** Jesus. For the law of **the Spirit of life has set you free in Christ Jesus from the law of sin and death**. For God has done what the law, weakened by the flesh, could not do. By sending his own Son in the likeness of sinful flesh and for sin, he condemned sin in the flesh, in order that **the righteous** requirement of the law might be fulfilled in us, **who walk not according to the flesh but according to the Spirit**. (Romans 8:1–4)*

Chapter 3.2

Freeing the Mind—Seeking a Mind above Thought

You have now found freedom within your mind, in the surrender or death of the captured thought that had led you to seek something outside the Presence of life. In its death, *in Christ*, you have now been set free within your mind. You have surrendered the thoughts that continue to seek beyond life in the now, and in your surrender you are seeking a mind's position that is above it. Your mind is now transcending above thoughts to a stillness within it. Your mind has found its right positioning, having surrendered to what is in the moment. You have come to an agreement through your satisfaction of life that is now occurring. You are in alignment with life's Presence for your thinking and seeking mind is no longer resisting life's reality. Your mind's positioning has been raised to a higher state of existing: that of a Conscious awareness of life's Presence in the now occurring.

You have been *raised with Christ*, your mind has been raised or transcended higher to its right position of Being fully Present and aware of life's Presence in the now. You are *seated*, or mentally positioned, having fully aligned with the natural flow of life's unfolding of itself. You are One with life again in your alignment or right position to your awareness of its reality of existence. You have died to the mind's searching for the things of the earth, and you have placed your mind above this thinking to a resting place of what is; a place of ease, of surrender to what is; this is a place of nonresistance to the natural flow of life in your awareness of its Presence of Being. You are not the thoughts you think, for you have surrendered them to a stillness of mind, a mind that is now in awareness of its Oneness with life.

Surrender your thoughts to Me! Become still within your mind to the awareness of the Presence of Being!

SURRENDERING YOUR THOUGHTS

Be Present! Come into the awareness of life, its true existence. Be Present, having fullness of mind to an awareness of life's unfolding of itself. Do you not see Me, this life that is now occurring? Do not allow your mind to seek outwardly from My Presence of Being, for nothing exists beyond this moment of life.

You are not the thoughts that arise within your mind, this false sense of self, this ego that has led you from a reality of life to an unreality of existence. For when you hold every thought captive to Christ, you transcend your mind to an awareness of just Being Present to life. You have risen above all thought to a right-standing position of Conscious awareness of what is.

Free the mind; embrace the Spirit!

Keep seeking that which is above thought to a stillness within your mind, a moment of rest and reprieve, and then you shall come into the awareness of the Presence of Being—One with life, One with Me.

$\mathcal{F}$REEDOM FOUND WITHIN IS THE SURRENDER OF THE THINKING AND RATIONALIZING MIND. FREEDOM IS FOUND IN THE MIND THAT CHOOSES TO LET GO AND RISE ABOVE THE IMPULSIVE THINKING.

But I am afraid that as the serpent deceived Eve by his cunning, **your thoughts will be led astray from a sincere and pure devotion to Christ**. *(2 Corinthians 11:3)*

Have this mind among yourselves, *which is* **yours in Christ** *Jesus …. (Philippians 2:5)*

If then you have been **raised with Christ**, **seek the things that are above**, *where Christ is, seated at the right hand of God.* **Set your minds on things that are above**, **not on things that are on earth**. *(Colossians 3:1–2)*

$\mathcal{Y}$OUR MIND'S RENEWAL IS THE SURRENDER OF THE THINKING, RATIONALIZING, AND SEEKING MIND, TO A MIND THAT IS STILL AND PRESENT THROUGH AN AWARENESS OF WHAT IS.

Do not be conformed to this world, *but* **be transformed by the renewal of your mind**, *that by testing* **you may discern what is the will of God**, *what is good and acceptable and perfect. (Romans 12:2)*

And to be **renewed in the spirit of your minds** *…. (Ephesians 4:23)*

> *For thus says the Lord to the house of Israel:*
> *"***Seek me and live** *…." (Amos 5:4)*

Chapter 3.3

Be Still and Know—You Are the Witness

In Stillness You Shall Know

We know that we are not our thoughts, having surrendered or died to them. We have risen above the thinking, rationalizing, and seeking mind. We were once deceived by the ego, the false self-awareness that had separated us from life's Presence. We have surrendered the impulsive seeking mind that had led us astray from Being Present in the now of life's reality. We have transcended in our mind's positioning to that which is above thought. Now, there is a stillness of mind, a mental reprieve from all its seeking and resisting life in the Present. You have now entered into a state of awareness of just Being alive in this moment, coming into an agreement with life's now occurring.

You Are the Witnessing Mind

In your state of awareness to Being Present of mind, still in thought and in agreement or alignment with what is, you are no longer the impulsive thinking, rationalizing, and seeking mind. You have now become the observing mind or the mind that is just witnessing life as it reveals itself. Your mind has come to a place of rest, a stillness, One with an awareness of Being Present; you are a witness to life in the Present moment of its existence. Your mind is now fully awake, alert and Present in its observing of life. You are fully Conscious and aware of life's occurring around you, and its life force energy within you giving you your very Being of aliveness. Your mind has now become the *observing witness* to life in your awareness of its reality.

Surrendering the False Self to Become One with Your True Self

Our identity of Oneness with life is found in the surrender of impulsive thoughts, for we are not the rationalizing or the seeking mind, as we once believed. We are not this false self-identity that we had created from our separation from life's Presence. In our stillness, we become the observer, the witness to life's Presence. We come into the light of awareness. *Be still and know that I am God.* Be still in the mind, and become aware of life's Presence, the existence of it within you, and the unfolding of itself all around you. You need only to be the observer or witness to life to become One with its Presence. You have become awakened to life through your stillness of Being only Present with it. Be still and know, for you are the observer, the witnessing Presence to life in your awareness of its now reality of existence. You are One with life, One with God, One with the observing, witnessing Presence.

You shall see Life! Its Presence shall be found! Yes, seek Him in the silence of your mind, and you shall be a witness also!

Through the mind's stillness, you will come into a Present state of mind to witness life's only reality.

SURRENDER YOUR THOUGHTS TO A SILENT, QUIET, AND STILL MIND.

Be still, **and know that I am God**. *(Psalm 46:10)*

The LORD *will fight for you, and* **you have only to be silent**. *(Exodus 14:14)*

*It is good that one should **wait quietly**
for the salvation of the* LORD. *(Lamentations 3:26)*

Wait for the LORD;
*be strong, and let your heart take courage;
wait for the* LORD! *(Psalm 27:14)*

*For God alone, O my soul, **wait in silence**,
for my hope is from him. (Psalm 62:5)*

O that you would be completely silent,
And that it would become your wisdom! (Job 13:5)

Blessed is the one who listens to me,
watching daily at my gates,
waiting beside my doors. *(Proverbs 8:34)*

*But **I have calmed and quieted my soul**,
like a weaned child with its mother;
like a weaned child is my soul within me.
(Psalm 131:2)*

*But **the** LORD *is in His **holy temple**.
Let all the earth **be silent before Him**.
(Habakkuk 2:20)*

> The Sovereign LORD has given me a well-instructed
>   tongue, to know the word that sustains the weary.
> **He wakens me morning by morning,**
>   **wakens my ear to listen like one being**
>   **instructed**. *(Isaiah 50:4)*

> For the evildoers shall be cut off,
>   **but those who wait for the LORD shall inherit**
>   **the land**. *(Psalm 37:9)*

*Y*OU COME INTO THE LIGHT OF AWARENESS THROUGH THE MIND'S STILLNESS. YOU BECOME THE OBSERVING, WITNESSING PRESENCE TO LIFE'S REALITY.

Witnesses to Jesus

I can do nothing on my own. **As I hear**, *I judge, and my judgment is just, because* **I seek not my own will but the will of him who sent me**. *If I alone bear witness about myself, my testimony is not true.* **There is another who bears witness about me**, *and I know that the testimony that he bears about me is true. You sent to John, and he has borne witness to the truth.* **Not that the testimony that I receive is from man**, *but I say these things so that you may be saved.* **He was a burning and shining lamp**, *and* **you were willing to rejoice for a while in his light**. *But the testimony that I have is greater than that of John.* **For the works that the Father has given me to accomplish**, **the very works that I am doing**, **bear witness about me that the Father has sent me**. **And the Father who sent me has himself borne witness about me**. **His voice you have never heard**, *his form you have never seen, and you do not have his word abiding in you,* **for you do not believe** *the one whom he has sent. You search the Scriptures because you think that in them you have eternal* life; and it is they that bear witness about me, **yet you refuse to come to me that you may have life.** *(John 5:30–40)*

But **you will receive power when the Holy Spirit has come upon you**, and you **will be my witnesses** in Jerusalem and in all Judea and Samaria, and to the end of the earth. *(Acts 1:8)*

Chapter 3.4

The Light of Awareness—You Have Entered through the Inner Room of Consciousness

You Are a Conscious Presence to Life's Existence

In the light of your awareness of Being One with life in the now of its existence, you have become the observing mind, the witnessing Presence to life in the now occurring. You have come into the light of awareness; you have come into *the inner room* of Consciousness. This is your awareness to life's abiding Presence within you and all around you. Your mind is in a Present and upright position of Being fully alert and aware of life's now occurring. You have reached a full Conscious awareness to life's unfolding Presence of itself, this here and now reality. You have reached a Conscious awareness of life itself, in your observing of it. You are the observer in your awareness of life's Presence of Being. You are God (life) Consciousness in your observing or awareness of life. You have transcended your mind to awareness, an enlightened state of observation, of witnessing life as it is. And within your awareness, your observing, your witnessing of its unfolding Presence, you become One with it, One with life, with God. You are God manifest, having become One through your Conscious awareness to the reality of life's existence. You are in the mind's right-standing position, its alignment or agreement with the Presence of life. As Jesus taught, *you are the light of life*, having an awareness to its abiding Presence within and all around you. You are the observing Conscious Presence to life itself.

*Y*OUR INNER ROOM

Come to a place of solitude, away from the world's distractions and seek Presence within your mind. And when you have hidden yourself, giving Me your thoughts and your desires, then be still. Allow your mind, its thoughts, to fall away from you to an inner quietness. Free your mind of thought to a mind's awareness of just Being here in the Present moment, with Me. You have taken your mind's attention off of the false self-awareness, what it desires and seeks, and have waited in the silence of your mind. Be still and know that I AM God. And in the mind's freedom from thought, I will manifest Myself to you! I AM in your inner room, your mind's Conscious awareness to the simple act of Being Present with Me. My Presence arises within your stillness of mind! Are you aware of Me, of life's existence by Being Present in this moment? This is life, child! You have entered in through your inner room, the inner room of Consciousness. You now have an awareness of life!

Let go of the world, hide from it! Seek the desolate places, those of solitude and silence, free from the distractions of this world. As you begin to release your thoughts, the desires that you are seeking from the world, you enter into a peaceful silence of the mind, and then … I AM! Through your mind's awakening, you become One with the Presence of Being.

Let your mind be still, and wait upon the awareness of Being Present with it! This is life in this Present moment of your awareness to its existence!

Enter the inner sanctuary. The Kingdom of God is within! Shall you not enter? Forgo the false self-awareness that experiences the external world, and seek the Conscious awareness of life's Presence that is found within you!

Retreat to the stillness of your thoughts and mind; quiet your self. Hide the false self to find fellowship with My Presence of Being.

$\mathcal{M}$ENTAL PREPAREDNESS

Surely as the sun sets in the sky, so have My eyes set upon you. Your all-knowing Father has not missed one single day of your life. My eyes have not left your very existence out of My sight. No, I have set My mind upon you, child. And in the distance, you have momentarily looked to Me. In your hesitancy you forsake My Presence, of Being One with life. Your day has a long list of what to do, and in your mind's seeking, you have left the Present moment of life's reality. Come, child, do not be hesitant. Come sit in My Presence, be still in your mind's seeking and surrender to Being One with life in this moment. Come, enjoy the vastness of life in your Present state of mind! You see, you and I are One, for you surrendered to life in the Present moment, and you have become One with just Being in the now. For My Presence is your very existence of life! I shall build you up and prepare you for the day, to assure you of the good blessings that are in store for you and to fill your very soul with gladness. I will fulfill you in all that you lack: joy, peace of mind, love, and contentment. They are yours in total surrender to My Presence. Let us face the horizon together as I have prepared the way. Remain in total surrender to life in the Present moment, for this is the way I have set out for you to follow. Shall you prepare your mind for its surrender to life? To what is in this moment? I await you!

What good is this world as you seek about and forgo the very Presence of life? You have lost the reality of life in your seeking beyond My Presence.

Don't be distracted by the world's seeking for more, but be Present in every moment of life.

$\mathcal{W}$AKE UP, SLEEPER!

Unbeknownst to you, I exist. You are unaware of My whole Being, yet you still exist. Why, oh why, sleeper, do you fail to know Me?

Why do you fail to know the hands that made you? For I have yet to call you from the deep sleep you exist in, unaware that your salvation is near. Wake up, sleeper, for your Father calls you. Arise to this very moment of awareness. Surrender your seeking mind to a stillness, and be Present to My Being of aliveness that moves through you! Wake up, sleeper, your mind has been caught up in its seeking, and you have fallen asleep to the Presence of Being alive in this moment.

You are dead to the Presence of Being alive. But now I have called you out of that slumber to the awareness of who you are in Me, and that I AM in you!

If you seek the world, you shall gain the world. If you seek Me within you, you shall gain the awareness of life! I AM the Conscious Being to life in the now, living life in this moment! Shall you not awaken to life in the Presence of My Being?

$\mathcal{H}$IDE YOURSELF (THE FALSE SELF-AWARENESS) AND ENTER INTO THE *INNER ROOM* (YOUR STATE OF CONSCIOUS AWARENESS) TO FIND LIFE'S PRESENCE.

*And Micaiah said, "Behold, **you shall see** on that day when you **go into an inner chamber** to **hide yourself**." (1 Kings 22:25)*

*But when you pray, **go into your room** and shut the door and pray to your Father who is in **secret**. And your Father who sees in secret will reward you. (Matthew 6:6)*

$\mathcal{A}$ PRESENT STATE OF MIND IS THE ANCHOR OF THE SOUL WHICH IS FOUND BEHIND THE CURTAIN OR THE VEIL THAT IS TORN (THE FALSE SELF-AWARENESS).

*We have this as a sure and **steadfast anchor** of the soul, a hope that **enters into the inner place** behind the curtain …. (Hebrews 6:19)*

$\mathcal{Y}$OU NOW HAVE THE LIGHT OF LIFE; THE MIND'S AWARENESS TO THE REALITY OF LIFE'S PRESENCE.

*Again Jesus spoke to them, saying, "**I am the light of the world. Whoever follows me will not walk in darkness**, but **will have the light of life**." (John 8:12)*

*For at one time you were darkness, but **now you are light in the Lord**. (Ephesians 5:8)*

*For **anything that becomes visible is light**.*
    Therefore it says,
*"**Awake, O sleeper**,*
        *and **arise from the dead**,*
*and **Christ will shine on you**." (Ephesians 5:14)*

*"While **you have the light**, believe in the light, that you may become **sons of light**." When Jesus had said these things, he departed and hid himself from them. (John 12:36)*

$\mathcal{Y}$OUR MIND'S RIGHT-STANDING POSITION (RIGHTEOUSNESS) IN THE STATE OF BEING A WITNESS OR OBSERVER OPENS THE MIND'S GATE TO THE AWARENESS OF LIFE'S PRESENCE.

Open to me the gates of righteousness,
   that I may enter through them
   and give thanks to the LORD.
This is the gate of the LORD;
   the righteous shall enter through it.
I thank you that you have answered me
   and **have become my salvation**.
   (Psalm 118:19-21)

$\mathcal{T}$HE AWAKENED MIND IS CONSCIOUSLY AWARE AND FULLY PRESENT TO LIFE'S OCCURRING IN THE NOW.

And to the angel of the church in Sardis write: "The words of him who has the seven spirits of God and the seven stars.

*"'I know your works. **You have the reputation of being alive, but you are dead. Wake up,** and **strengthen what remains and is about to die**, for I have not found your works complete in the sight of my God. Remember, then, what you received and heard. Keep it, **and repent. If you will not wake up**, I will come like a thief, and you will not know at what hour I will come against you." (Revelation 3:1–3)*

*Besides this you know **the time**, that the hour **has come** for you **to wake from sleep. For salvation is nearer to us** now than when we first believed. (Romans 13:11)*

*Behold! I tell you a mystery. **We shall not all sleep**, but **we shall all be changed**. (1 Corinthians 15:51)*

*But in fact **Christ has been raised from the dead, the first fruits of those who have fallen asleep**. (1 Corinthians 15:20)*

***But stay awake at all times**, praying that you may have strength to escape all these things that are going to take place, and to stand before the Son of Man. (Luke 21:36)*

Chapter 3.5

In and Out of Pasture—Entering into a Present Moment State of Awareness

Going In and Out of a Conscious Awareness to Life's Presence

You now know the way to the Kingdom of God—your awareness to the existence of life found only in the Present moment through a Present state of mind. This is a continual practice of entering a state of Conscious awareness to Being Present and One with life in the now. It is a continual surrender of the impulsive thinking, seeking, and rationalizing mind, to become still and enter into a state of Conscious awareness of life's Presence. This is the true reality of life's existence in the here and now. You are One with life, having your mind in a right standing or aligned position, coming into an agreement with life's unfolding of itself in this moment.

Experiencing the Kingdom of God is a continual practice or *renewing of the mind* to surrender impulsive thoughts and desires; a continual practice of entering into a state of Conscious awareness of Being fully Present in the now of life's reality. We have found enlightenment, for we have entered into the awareness of life's only existence. We have not mentally resisted life's Presence, yet we have surrendered and have become One with its now occurring. We are observing life in complete silence and stillness, fully aware and alert about what is now happening. In our moments of Conscious awareness, we enter into a mental reprieve, a rest; as Jesus metaphorically teaches, we can go in and out to find pasture. God, the life force energy and our Conscious awareness of its Presence within, is referred to as pasture. We are the sheep of life, and we find the pasture (Presence of life) when we are fully immersed in the here and now of reality, the Present moment. As the Psalm of David says, He makes us lie down in green pastures. There is a peace and ease of what is when you no longer resist life in the Present moment of its reality.

$\mathcal{L}$ONGING FOR PRESENCE

Without You, oh Lord, I am nothing. I cannot exist without Your Being, the life energy that moves through me. Yet in my straying from You, I long for Your Presence, so I shall come back to my mind's awareness of life in this moment! I will seek You for truth, direction, and guidance. I shall wait at Your gates, in right standing to my awareness of life's Presence. I shall long for You until you reveal Yourself. Yes, I shall seek You both day and night, surrendering myself fully to this Present moment of life. And You will reward Your faithful servant who waits at Your door patiently. For I have drawn near to the Present moment of Being One with life, One with You, in all of its existence, and You, dear life, have drawn Yourself to me. Yes, I am aware of You now! I shall be fully Present to Your unfolding!

$\mathcal{W}$E ARE THE SHEEP OF GOD'S PASTURE—OUR MIND'S PRESENT STATE OF AWARENESS TO LIFE IN THE NOW.

Know that the LORD*, he is **God**!*
*It is **he who made us, and we are his;***
we are his people, and the sheep of his
***pasture**. (Psalm 100:3)*

$\mathcal{M}$ETAPHORICALLY SPEAKING JESUS REFERS TO DEATH OF THE EGO OR FALSE SELF-AWARENESS AS HIMSELF. YOU ENTER INTO THE PRESENT STATE OF MIND OR PASTURE THROUGH THE DOOR OR GATE (THE DEATH OF THE FALSE SELF-AWARENESS).

*I am the door. If anyone enters by me, he will be saved and will **go in and out and find pasture**. (John 10:9)*

*That **times of refreshing** may **come from the presence** of the Lord, and that he may send the Christ appointed for you, Jesus, whom heaven must receive until the time for restoring all the things about which God spoke by the mouth of his holy prophets long ago. (Acts 3:20–21)*

Surely the righteous shall give thanks to your name;
***the upright shall dwell in your presence**.*
(Psalm 140:13)

$\mathcal{T}$HE EGO SURRENDERS INTO A STILL AND PEACEFUL PASTURE (A PRESENT STATE OF MIND).

*He makes me lie down in **green pastures**.*
*He leads me beside **still waters**. (Psalm 23:2)*

Chapter 4

Your Mind's Alignment with the Reality of Life's Presence – You Are Now One with the Creator of All Existence

Chapter 4.1

Salvation—You Have Reached the End of Your Mental Suffering

In the light of awareness, you have surrendered your seeking mind. The ego's drama and false self-awareness, which had led your mind astray from the Presence of life, exists no more. There is no more mental torment, fear, doubt, worry, shame, and regret; it has all been left behind, having been put to death and ceased from its deceptive portrayal of life's existence. This false awareness of life has lied, pulling you away from the light of awareness to what is. You have suffered in a mental darkness, being pulled into an unconscious state of mind, unaware of life's true existence. You were once suffering in the ego's emotional pull, its condemnation, anger, jealousy, and insecurity, the state of mind that continually rationalized and sought after anything and everything that took you away from this moment of life's existence.

The ego mind was always discontented with just Being One with life in an awareness of it. The ego, the mind's enemy, is *the father of all lies*, as Jesus stated, lurking in hopes of devouring you. The mind, having fallen from the state of a Conscious awareness of what is, experiences a confused, unreal perception of life's existence. Yet, in your alert, wakeful and Present mind, you have become aware of the true reality of life. And all that the ego's pain has caused you, in your unawareness to life, has fallen away, and you are now Present in the light of awareness to life's only existence. Your mind has come back home to its rightful Present state of mind.

Bring all mental suffering to the light of awareness to life's Presence in the now; come into a fully Present state of mind to life's occurring in this moment. Your mind has reached a salvation, a place of rest and stillness, free from confusion and darkness, for you see things as they really are. Nothing exists beyond the reality of now, this Present moment of existence. The veil of deceit has been removed; the ego, the false self, has been put to death. You now have come into the light of awareness of what is reality, and the darkness, the unawareness, has left you. You have reached a moment of salvation, the end of the mind's suffering.

$\mathcal{E}$NLGHTENED TO THE PRESENCE OF LIFE

Those who call upon the Lord shall not be turned away. No, His Presence shall be upon them. In all His might and splendor, He shall make Himself known to them.

I see My servant lying at My footstool with his eyes up to heaven. I hear him cry out to Me, and surely, I will come in an instant. Surely, My Spirit shall be upon him. I will not leave him alone in this place. I will come to him in his darkness and make Myself known to him. I shall bring My light of awareness to him, and he will see life, its existence and true reality.

Once you taste the salvation that the Lord brings with Presence, you shall look for Him all day long. Yes, you will seek more of the God who brings you out of the depths of your torment and into His great light of awareness. Salvation belongs to all who call upon the name of the Lord. Do not hesitate! Call out to Him, your Conscious awareness of life in this moment, and experience life's abiding Presence. You have come to the end of your suffering!

In my despair, I cry out to You, and You will make Your Presence known to me! You will save me from the mental pain I endure! Yes, O God, You will rescue me from my mental torment, and the salvation of life's reality, its existence, shall be my crowning victory!

UNMISTAKABLE PRESENCE

The more you remain in Me, this Present moment of life's existence, the more I will pull you away from the world. The more you seek My Presence, the less you desire for things of this world. Your desires of this world wash away in My Presence. The things of the world will not matter to you anymore. They have no hold on you in the fullness of life's existence. And then it will be more of Me that you desire, a longing for solitude, to find rest in the stillness of life's unfolding. It will be My voice that you seek to hear. It will be My fountain of wisdom that you desire to flow. It will be My comfort and peace that you desire to experience. It will be My joy and gladness that you desire to fill your heart. You will desire more and more of Me. Do not look for Me outside of your inner awareness, for you will see that I am not in the world or of the world. My unmistakable Presence of life exists within you, your heart's longing and desire for Presence, this Oneness with life!

$\mathcal{S}$ALVATION IS FOUND IN THE MIND'S SURRENDERING OF THE FALSE SELF-AWARENESS THAT EXISTS OUTSIDE THE REALITY OF LIFE'S PRESENCE.

*For God did not send his Son into the world to condemn the world, but **in order that the world might be saved through him**. Whoever believes in him is not condemned, but whoever does not believe is condemned already, because he has not believed in the name of the only Son of God. And this is the judgment: **the light has come into the world**, and **people loved the darkness rather than the light** because their works were evil. For everyone who does wicked things hates the light and does not come to the light, lest his works should be exposed. But **whoever does what is true comes to the light**, so that it may be clearly seen that **his works have been carried out in God**. (John 3:17–21)*

$\mathcal{T}$HE SALVATION OF GOD IS WHEN YOU BECOME PRESENT OF MIND TO THE AWARENESS (LISTENING, OBSERVING, QUIET STATE) OF LIFE'S REALITY EXISTING IN THE NOW.

*Therefore let it be known to you that **this salvation of God** has been sent to the Gentiles; **they will listen**. (Acts 28:28)*

> **My soul also is greatly troubled**.
>   But you, O LORD—how long?
> Turn, O **Lord**, **deliver my life**;
>   **save me** for the sake of your **steadfast** love.
>   (Psalm 6:3–4)

> **Lead me in your truth** and teach me,
>   for you are **the God of my salvation**;
>   **for you I wait** all the day long. (Psalm 25:5)

To open their eyes, so that they may **turn from darkness to light** and from the power of Satan to God, that they may receive *forgiveness of sins and a place among those who are sanctified by faith in me. (Acts 26:18)*

$\mathcal{T}$HROUGH THE RIGHT STANDING POSTION OF YOUR MIND (A PRESENT STATE) YOU ARE SAVED FROM THE TORMENT OF THE DARKENED (UNAWARE) MIND. THE PRESENT STATE OF MIND IS THE STRONGHOLD, THE REFUGE, A VERY PRESENT HELP.

*The **salvation of the righteous is from the** L*ORD*;*
*he is their **stronghold** in the time of trouble.*
> *(Psalm 37:39)*

*God is our **refuge** and strength,*
> *a **very present help** in trouble. (Psalm 46:1)*

***For God alone** my soul **waits in silence**;*
> ***from him comes my salvation**. (Psalm 62:1)*

$\mathcal{R}$ETURNING (REPENT) IS TO COME BACK TO A PRESENT STATE OF MIND.

*For thus said the Lord G*OD*, the Holy One of Israel,*
*"**In returning and rest you shall be saved**;*
> ***in quietness** and **in trust** shall be your strength."*
But you were unwilling …. (Isaiah 30:15)

*For I am not ashamed of the gospel, for it is **the power of God for salvation** to **everyone who believes**, to the Jew first and also to the Greek. (Romans 1:16)*

*For to this end we toil and strive, because **we have our hope set on the living God**, who **is the Savior of all people, especially of those who believe**. (1 Timothy 4:10)*

For the grace of God has appeared, bringing salvation for all people. *(Titus 2:11)*

> The L*ORD* your God is **in your midst**,
>   a mighty one who **will save**;
> he will rejoice over you with gladness;
>   **he will quiet you** by his love;
> he will exult over you with loud singing. *(Zephaniah
>   3:17)*

For the word of the cross is folly to those who are perishing, **but to us who are being saved it is the power of God**. *(1 Corinthians 1:18)*

> **Salvation belongs to the L*ORD*;**
> your blessing be on your people! Selah. *(Psalm 3:8)*

> **His glory is great through your salvation;**
>   splendor and majesty you bestow on him. *(Psalm
>   21:5)*

That times of refreshing may come from the presence of the Lord, and that he may send the Christ appointed for you, Jesus, whom heaven must receive until the time for restoring all the things about which God spoke by the mouth of his holy prophets long ago. *(Acts 3:20–21)*

> **And my spirit rejoices in God my Savior,**
> **for he has looked on the humble estate of his**
>   **servant**.
>   For behold, from now on all generations will call
>   me blessed …. *(Luke 1:47–48)*

Chapter 4.2

The Peace That Surpasses All Understanding

In the death of your ego, you have reached salvation. The mind is still; it has come to a place of rest and ease, fully surrendered to life in this moment. You are no longer living in darkness, an unreal version of life's existence, the unawareness of it; you are now living in the light of awareness of life, life in the now occurring. Your ego with its false awareness of reality, its illusion to seek outside the existence of life, no longer enslaves your mind. You are no longer subject to confusion about what is real or to the fear, anxiety, agitation, or conflict within. You have surrendered these thoughts to the stillness of a quiet mind, a calm mind, free of thought. And in your stillness, your silence, you step into the light of awareness of Being.

You are no longer the thinking mind but the observing mind, fully surrendered to witnessing life in its now of unfolding. You are no longer resisting life yet you have come into an agreement with the reality of its existence, this Present Moment of time. You have been reconciled, brought back to the Oneness of life's true existence in the now. You are One with life as you witness its flow of energy in and around you. You are now fully restored, in the correct position of your mind, having aligned yourself with the awareness of Being Present to life's true existence. You have entered into a peaceful calmness, a quietness of mind, the still mind that only observes this natural flow of life. You are not in resistance to life, but have come into an alignment with it. You have an inner peaceful disposition, a freedom of mind. This is a state of happiness, blissfulness, and contentment. You are in harmony with what is, life in its only existence, the Present moment of reality. You are One with life in your awareness of it, your observing of it.

In the light of your awareness of life's true existence, you have surrendered to a trust of what is: this natural flow of life energy that is in all and through all. It is a complete surrender to a peaceful disposition that surpasses any thought or conceptualization of what is. You no longer need to think or bring reason. You just need to surrender the mind to a stillness of what is. This is the peace that surpasses all understanding; it surpasses any mind's reasoning to an acceptance of what is now occurring.

In an unreal perception of life, there is no rest. There is confusion, discord, conflict, and disturbance. Your mind is in resistance to life's truth. It has left life's Presence and entered into an illusion of what is.

The mind that has transcended thought to a stillness of Being is free! It has left behind its resistance of life in the now to a peaceful surrender. It is no longer the thinking and reasoning mind of understanding; it has stepped into the light of awareness of what is. That mind is now the observing, witnessing mind to life's unfolding. It has become One with the reality of life's existence.

Experience the fruit of the surrendered mind: overwhelming peace and contentment, regardless of any situation or circumstance in life! Your mind has surrendered its reasoning to the peace of what is.

All suffering exists within the false self-awareness. Suffering is not living in the reality or the awareness of what is.

Let go of the self, the ego, the reasoning and thinking mind, and let peace overcome you in your surrender to what is!

$\mathcal{B}$ECOMING ONE WITH PEACE

In the stillness of my mind, I find You there. Through complete surrender of the false self-awareness that I have created, its focus and desires, I find You. Oh Lord! For a complete moment,

I have found Your Presence within me. Within my Conscious awareness, You exist! And You have always been there, only to my indifference, I have put my self above You! If just for a moment I can be still to the thoughts of my self and surrender this false self-awareness, I shall become One with You! I have found and tasted the Eternal Presence that abides within me. I have found my true identity! You are in me, Lord, and I am in You! And in the Oneness, I have let go of the struggle I have with You! Yes, I have accepted You, life as it is in this very moment! And my search has not failed me! No, You are a constant Eternal Presence, this free flowing life energy, this living water, and You have always remained with me, since the moment You brought me into existence.

I cannot live without the life force that is within me! Yet it has been I who chose to hang on to this false awareness of what is, the false self-identity, the ego! And when I become one with this false awareness, I have forsaken You, the Presence of life itself! I have created my own struggle and mental torment, for the false self, the pride, the ego, leads only to my destruction and pain. It takes me out of the reality of life, found in this Present moment, to a death experience, life that does not exist. I have fallen from my awareness to life's true existence in this Present moment! I shall rise up again, dear Lord! I shall seek Your Presence for the surrender of my mental anguish, for I have strayed too far from Your Presence and into my own! I have turned my mind's focus from You to the illusion of something beyond. And therein lies my torment, the darkness of the pit that I have chosen to fall into!

I shall turn my intentions and self-focus back to You! I shall come back home to You, the Giver of Eternal life, and I shall find peace because I have given up on the struggle to go against You! Yes, I have surrendered to You, life in this moment, and Your Presence within me! And once I surrender all resistance to what is, then I shall find my mind's peace! Free from mental torment and anguish, confusion and fear, the darkness that has enveloped me, I shall become One with You, in my mind's agreement with what is. Peace will surround me when I have surrendered in my battle with You, Oh Lord, and have come into Your Presence of Being.

I surrender, Oh Lord! I surrender this war I have waged in defiance of You, and I shall come back to You! I shall become One with life's existence in the now!

Free your mind! Surrender your thoughts to come into an awareness of life's existence in the now. Come into the peace of the still mind through the witnessing of life's unfolding. There is peace of mind in the observing of life, your awareness of it. The mind has settled and is now only observing.

THE PRESENCE OF PEACE EMERGES THROUGH THE SURRENDERED EGOIC MIND OF RATIONALIZING (UNDERSTANDING).

*And **the peace of God**, which **surpasses all understanding**, **will guard** your hearts and **your minds in Christ** Jesus. (Philippians 4:7)*

THE EGO HAS CREATED AN ILLUSION TO LEAD THE MIND AWAY FROM LIFE IN THE PRESENT MOMENT. SURRENDER THE THINKING AND REASONING MIND TO AN AWARENESS OF LIFE'S PRESENCE IN THE HERE AND NOW.

*I have said these things to you, **that in me you may have peace**. **In the world you will have tribulation**. But take heart; **I have overcome the world**. (John 16:33)*

*For to set **the mind on the flesh is death**, but to **set the mind on the Spirit is life and peace**. (Romans 8:6)*

> ***You keep him in perfect peace***
> ***whose mind is stayed on you**,*
> *because **he trusts** in you. (Isaiah 26:3)*

*And **let the peace of Christ rule in your hearts**, to which indeed you were called in one body. And **be thankful**. (Colossians 3:15)*

*Therefore, since we have been **justified by faith, we have peace with God through our Lord Jesus Christ**. (Romans 5:1)*

COME INTO AN AGREEMENT WITH LIFE'S REALITY OF EXISTENCE THROUGH THE MIND'S WITNESSING OR OBSERVING OF LIFE'S PRESENCE IN THE NOW.

> **Agree with God, and be at peace;**
> thereby good will come to you. (Job 22:21)

𝒴OU HAVE BEEN BROUGHT INTO THE LIGHT
OF AWARENESS THROUGH A MIND THAT IS
WITNESSING LIFE AS IT IS, IN THIS MOMENT.
YOU TRUST REALITY AS YOU SEE IT AND NO
LONGER FEAR THE ILLISION OF UNKNOWNS.

Peace I leave with you; my peace I give to you. Not as the
world gives do I give to you. **Let not your hearts be troubled,
neither let them be afraid**. (John 14:27)

𝒯HERE IS PEACE FOUND WITHIN THE OBSERVING
MIND; FOR IT HAS TRANSCENDED OR RISEN ABOVE
IT'S THINKING AND REASONING OF WHAT COULD OR
OUGHT TO BE, TO A HIGHER STATE OF OBSERVING
WHAT IS ACTUALLY OCCURRING IN THE NOW.

> **Glory to God in the highest**,
> and on earth **peace among those with whom he is
> pleased**! (Luke 2:14)

𝒯HERE IS TRUST THROUGH YOUR AWARENESS
OF LIFE'S REALITY, FOR YOU SEE IT AS IT IS. THERE
IS NO CONFUSION ABOUT WHAT IS REAL.

And the effect of righteousness will be peace,
and the **result of righteousness, quietness and trust forever**.
(Isaiah 32:17)

> Behold, God **is my salvation;**
> **I will trust, and will not be afraid**;
> for the LORD GOD is my strength and my song,
> and **he has become my salvation**. (Isaiah 12:2)

So flee youthful passions and **pursue righteousness**, faith, love, and **peace**, along with **those who call on the Lord** from a pure heart. *(2 Timothy 2:22)*

For **the kingdom of God** is not a matter of eating and drinking but of **righteousness** and **peace** and joy **in the Holy Spirit**. *(Romans 14:17)*

> **He enters into peace**;
> **they rest in their beds**
> who walk in their **uprightness**. *(Isaiah 57:2)*

The latter glory of this house shall be greater than the former, says the LORD of hosts. **And in this place I will give peace**, declares the LORD of hosts. *(Haggai 2:9)*

YOU ARE ONE WITH LIFE; NO LONGER RESISTING A PRESENT STATE OF MIND TO BEING ONE WITH IT.

Eager to maintain the **unity of the Spirit in the bond of peace**. *(Ephesians 4:3)*

My people will abide in a peaceful habitation, in **secure dwellings**, and **in quiet resting places**. *(Isaiah 32:18)*

Chapter 4.3

You Are Complete—Receiving the Crown of Life

You have risen above your false self-awareness, having died to the ego's seeking thoughts for more than what is. You have surrendered the thinking and rationalizing mind to a silence, a stillness of thought, and you have now entered into the light of awareness. You are no longer the thinking mind; you are now the observing or witnessing mind. You are without the mind's active thought and have surrendered to a position of Being aware of life as it is in its unfolding of itself. You have momentarily overcome the world, the mind that seeks for more beyond the Presence of life, and have surrendered to a mind that is just in awareness of life itself. You are simply noticing or perceiving the flow of life, its life energy, moving and Being through you and around you. You have reached the light of awareness, having been enlightened to the witnessing or observing to life's Presence. Your mind has reached an awareness of life's natural flow and existence in the here and now of time. Your journey has been completed, you have nothing further to seek. You are here, witnessing life in its expression of itself. You are One with life in your complete awareness of it. You are the witnessing Presence to life. Your mind is in alignment, in its right standing position of Being Present, fully Conscious, awake and aware, silently observing. Now that you have completed your mind's journey, you have been crowned the gift of life. In your completion, you see the reality of life as it is, in the now of its existing Presence.

The Crown of Life

The crown of life is your awareness to life's Presence within you and all around you. Your mind is no longer fixed on the limited false-self awareness; rather, it has now opened up and expanded to a larger awareness of what is reality. The crown of life or God Consciousness is your full perspective, unlimited focus and attention to what is now occurring in the Presence of life. You have overcome the ego's mind, the trials and unrest it brings to a stillness within the mind; the mind's observance to life itself. The mind has surrendered and has come into an accord with what is actually happening in the now.

Jesus said the devil will throw you into prison to be tested (the mind that is caught up by the ego's drama; the mind that is not aware of life's Presence), but you are to be faithful unto death (death of the ego mind or surrendering your false-self awareness), and He will give you the crown of life (through your surrender of the false self, your death, your mind has now opened up to the witnessing of life's Presence in the now of reality).

We have successfully finished the race to find life, our journey now complete. Having surrendered the false self-awareness, we have let go of our thinking and doing, and instead we are witnessing and observing life. We have come into the light of awareness of life, having been a witness to its existence, the here and now. We are fulfilled, having completed the race and have received the crown of life.

*T*HROUGH THE DEATH OF YOUR SELF-AWARENESS YOU HAVE COMPLETED THE JOURNEY AND HAVE RECEIVED THE GIFT OR THE REALIZATION THAT LIFE'S EXISTENCE IS ONLY FOUND IN THE MIND'S PRESENT STATE OF AWARENESS TO IT.

*Jesus said to him, "**I am the way, and the truth, and the life. No one comes to the Father except through me**." (John 14:6)*

And when the chief Shepherd appears, you will receive the unfading crown of glory. *(1 Peter 5:4)*

*T*HE THIEF IS THE EGO, ROBBING THE MIND OF LIFE'S REALITY.

The thief comes only to steal and kill and destroy. I came that they may have life and have it abundantly. *(John 10:10)*

An athlete is not crowned *unless he* **competes according to the rules.** *(2 Timothy 2:5)*

*R*EMAINING STEADFAST OR PRSENT OF MIND TO RECEIVE THE CROWN OF LIFE.

*Blessed is the man who **remains steadfast under trial**, for **when he has stood the test he will receive the crown of life**, which God has promised to those who love him. (James 1:12)*

Do not fear what you are about to suffer. *Behold,* **the devil is about to throw some of you into prison,** *that* **you may be tested**, *and for ten days you will have tribulation.* **Be faithful unto death, and I will give you the crown of life.** *(Revelation 2:10)*

*Henceforth there is laid up for me **the crown of righteousness**, which the Lord, the righteous judge, will **award to me on that***

Day*, and not only to me but also* **to all who have loved his appearing***. (2 Timothy 4:8)*

> **They cast their crowns before the throne***, saying,*
> *"****Worthy are you, our Lord and God***,*
>   *to receive glory and honor and power,*
> **for you created all things,**
>   **and by your will they existed and were**
>   **created***." (Revelation 4:10–11)*

Chapter 4.4

The Power of Discernment

The mind's discernment or the ability to spiritually judge well, is through the mind's Conscious awareness to life's unfolding reality. Your mind is alert and awake, Present to the observing or witnessing of life in the now. Your mind is clear of thought, fully in position, prepared to receive clarity of Consciousness. You are no longer the ego mind, the seeking, rationalizing and judging mind through the false-self awareness, but you now have God Consciousness through the awareness of Spirit, the breath, the life flow energy within and all around you. You have come to a Present state of mind, and you are now the observer to life, seeing exactly the way things are, the reality of life's Presence. In your light of awareness you are keen, finely sharpened to the perception of the now occurring of life. In your alertness you are spiritually sensitive to all that is around you. This is your clarity of Consciousness, the ability to judge well, having seen the reality of what is before you. And because you are alert, fully awake and Present, the mind is capable of receiving the natural flow of wisdom and understanding through Consciousness. You have the capability to discern all things, having understanding and wisdom through the alertness or the awareness of what is in front of you. Your mind is not distracted by thoughts but has become the listening and observing mind, fully awake in the light of your awareness. You know the direction in which you are going; life is fully Present in front of you, unfolding before your very eyes.

You have the power and the ability to receive wisdom, understanding, insight, and clarity through the mind that is fully Present, Consciously aware of the here and now. You are One with life, the Creator of all things, the Divine Intelligence; you are One with the flow of Omniscience. In your awareness, you know all, for nothing is hidden from you. The truth is right in front of you; it is Present in this moment, through your mind's awareness of its existence.

I have searched for You. Secluded from the world's distractions, I sought You out, dear Lord! And You came to me! With great revelation and truth, You spoke to me! Oh, what wisdom You have bestowed upon me! Oh, how I have come to know You, the Great Eternal God, Your Conscious Being that is within me!

I shall tell you of mysteries, treasures, and revelations; write them down so that you know these are from Me because I have already told you of them before they are to happen.

𝒯HE KEY OF AWARENESS UNLOCKS THE DOOR TO UNDERSTANDING

Surrender your false self-awareness to Me, My Presence of life in this moment. Have faith, trusting what is in this moment of reality. I shall give you intuition beyond your mind's rationalizing. In your awareness, I shall give you great insight to guide you. Lend an ear to Me, sit in the silence of your mind, and wait to hear My voice. You may dwell in wisdom for all your life's existence and I will freely give it to you. Is not your awareness of life's reality of this moment the truth of what is? Do you not see life in your observing of it? What is to rationalize or to try to understand for your self? Do you not see it as it is? Don't let your mind stray from My Presence. Remain Present and aware of life's existence, and My wisdom and understanding will continue to flow within you. Seek My wisdom found in your awareness of life's Presence, and you shall gain understanding of what is! Wake up, sleeper, and come alive in this Present moment of Being aware of life! Come sit with Me awhile. I have much to share with you.

$\mathcal{I}$NFINITE WISDOM

Come sit, child, there is much to tell you. Am I all infinite knowledge and wisdom? Surely, I AM. I AM the fountain of such truth. Then abide in Me, and what glorious truths shall be known to you. You see, I AM the Giver of Life, of Consciousness and Being. I AM your Life, your existence, I AM your Consciousness, your awareness, and I AM your Being of aliveness. All that exists, exists in Me. No other can give life, and no other shall take it. It is I who set the last decree. Seek Me for wisdom and understanding. Come forth and ask, and surely you will receive My innermost thoughts. I want to be One with you in Spirit. But that is your choice, to draw near to Me. Surely as the days go by, I shall remain a constant in your life, immovable. I AM here, in this Present moment and I will never leave you nor forsake you. Shall you never leave nor forsake Me? Even in all the days I have given you, I have not left your side for one of them. I have witnessed all of them.

$\mathcal{W}$ISDOM ABOUNDS

Wisdom abounds in your moment of stillness. Having no self-awareness, you have surrendered the mind's thinking and seeking for more. You have now rested your mind and have found peace within. You must shut out the world, all its distractions that lead you away from Being One with life's Presence, One with Me. I AM in the Present moment of your stillness of only Being Present and aware of what is.

Wisdom will abound in you. My thoughts shall inspire you, the quickening thought of great clarity and understanding. I shall exult over you with great influence! Wisdom is My communication to you, of great judgment to what is. For you will not need to reason anything, but I shall give you immediate understanding! It shall be swift, quick, and just, this moment of Conscious clarity. I shall pierce your Consciousness and give you truth and precision of what is.

For the light of awareness has shone on this new day, and you shall be My witness of Presence. Be still of mind now, and come into this awareness. I await you, having anticipated your return.

In the Presence of God, the awareness of life in this Present moment, the fountain of wisdom of Conscious clarity overflows. Through your awareness, He will open your eyes to the truth of what you did not see.

Become fully alive and awake in life's awareness! In truth, and in understanding, you shall see the reality of what is. I AM the Divine within; become fully awake in My Presence! All is given freely, don't you see? All is given freely to those who are awake and aware of Me! Seek, and you shall find, for I will give you insight into what you question. Ask, and it shall be given to you, for I will not keep one thing hidden from the mind that is fully aware of Me! I AM wisdom, and I AM understanding in your awareness to life's existence in this moment. Wake up the sleeping mind, and come into the light of awareness to what is before you!

*Y*OU HAVE TRANSCENDED RISING ABOVE RATIONAL THOUGHT TO A PRESENT STATE OF MIND; YOU ARE ONE WITH DIVINE WISDOM.

But the wisdom from above is first pure, then peaceable, gentle, open to reason, full of mercy and good fruits, impartial and sincere. (James 3:17)

That the God of our Lord Jesus Christ, the Father of glory, **may give you a spirit of wisdom and of revelation in the knowledge of him**, having the eyes of **your hearts enlightened**, that you may know what is the hope to which he has called you, what are the riches of his glorious inheritance in the saints .... (Ephesians 1:17–18)

> Surely I was sinful at birth,
>   sinful from the time my mother conceived me.
> Yet **you desired faithfulness** even in the womb;
>   **you taught me wisdom in that secret place**.
>   (Psalm 51:5–6 NIV)

Then **he opened their minds to understand** the Scriptures .... (Luke 24:45)

*T*HE POWER OF DISCERNMENT IS THROUGH THE ABILITY TO SEE OR BE AWARE OF THE REALITY OF LIFE AS IT IS SET OUT BEFORE YOU.

But solid food is for the mature, for those who have their **powers of discernment trained by constant practice** to distinguish good from evil. (Hebrews 5:14)

The natural person does not accept the things of the Spirit of God, for they are folly to him, and he is not able to understand them because they are **spiritually discerned**. (1 Corinthians 2:14)

$\mathcal{H}$AVING REVERENCE, TAKING HEED OR NOTICE, (FEAR) IS THE AWARENESS OF LIFE'S REALITY THROUGH THE OBSERVING AND PRESENT STATE OF MIND. IN THIS STATE YOU GAIN INSIGHT (AWARENESS) TO WHAT IS REAL.

The **fear of the LORD** is the **beginning of wisdom**,
and the **knowledge** of the Holy One is **insight**.
   (Proverbs 9:10)

Making your ear attentive to wisdom
      and **inclining your heart to understanding**;
yes, **if you call out for insight**
      and **raise your voice for understanding**,
if you seek it like silver
      and search for it as for hidden treasures,
then you will understand the fear of the Lord
      and find the knowledge of God.
   (Proverbs 2:2–5)

Daniel answered and said:

   "**Blessed be the name of God forever and ever,**
      to whom belong wisdom and might.
   He changes times and seasons;
      he removes kings and sets up kings;
   he gives wisdom to the wise
      and knowledge to those who have
      understanding;
   he reveals deep and hidden things …."
      (Daniel 2:20–22)

In whom are hidden all the treasures of wisdom and knowledge. *(Colossians 2:3)*

For **the Lord gives wisdom;**
   from his mouth come **knowledge and**
   understanding …. *(Proverbs 2:6)*

Wisdom *is with the aged,*
   and **understanding** *in length of days.*
With God are wisdom *and might;*
   he has **counsel and understanding.** *(Job*
   12:12–13)

If any of you lacks wisdom, let him ask God, *who gives* **generously to all** *without reproach, and* **it will be given him.** *(James 1:5)*

Blessed is the one who finds wisdom,
   and **the one who gets understanding,**
for the gain from her is better than gain from silver
   and her profit better than gold. (Proverbs 3:13–14)

Think over what I say, **for the Lord will give you understanding in everything.** *(2 Timothy 2:7)*

$\mathcal{B}$E OF A STILL MIND AND LISTEN; BE FULLY PRESENT AND ALERT TO HEAR.

An intelligent heart acquires knowledge,
   and **the ear of the wise seeks knowledge.**
   (Proverbs 18:15)

Call to me and I will answer you, *and will* **tell you great and hidden things that you have not known.** *(Jeremiah 33:3)*

And your ears shall hear *a word behind you, saying,* **"This is the way, walk in it**,*" when you turn to the right or when you turn to the left. (Isaiah 30:21)*

THE EYE OF AWARENESS; COME INTO THE LIGHT OF REALITY.

*I will instruct you and teach you in the way you
should go;
I will counsel you with my eye upon you.
(Psalm 32:8)*

Chapter 4.5

The Abundant Life—The Joy of Being One with Life's Presence

All Things Are Added to You through the Mind's Present State of Awareness

Your mind has surrendered to an awareness of the Presence of life in the now. You have surrendered all thought to an observing and witnessing mind, coming into your alignment or agreement with life's existence, your Present awareness of it. You have made peace within your mind to a surrender to what is, life's existence in this Present moment. You are embracing, interacting, engaging into the Oneness of this free flowing life force energy, this living water that moves in and around you, giving you your Being and aliveness. It is gentle and steady, naturally occurring; it is a position of trust for you see all things as they are, this reality of life in your Conscious awareness to it. There is a feeling of love and acceptance in your joining and Oneness with it. You are content and joyful and all things feel good and right through your inner Being of aliveness. You have clarity and perception to what is truth as you are a witness to it. Nothing is clouded, but you see things just as they are. It is reliable and trusted, it is reality. Therefore, you are patient with its unfolding of itself. You are secure, confident, strengthened in your knowledge of who you are, your true identity, this Oneness with life itself. You are in the light of life, your awareness to life's true existence in this Present moment. There is nothing to fear, worry, or doubt, for you see the truth of what is. You have left the death experience of unconscious unawareness to the reality of life, and the illusion of what was created has been completely forgiven, forgotten, as it never existed. Illusions never exist in the moment of awareness to reality. You are in the complete fullness and richness of life, its only reality of existence, this here and now Presence of life.

Life, at its abundance, begins with your awareness of Me! I will encourage, strengthen, and empower you to become all that I destined you to be.

Be Content with What You Have: A Continual Practice of the Mind to Ground in Presence

The ego, through its seeking and wanting for more than what is now occurring in life's Presence, leads your mind's awareness astray from enjoying life's reality. Jesus taught that if we were content with what we had, we would be grounded in this moment of life's Presence; for the Present moment of life's existence never leaves us; it is always here. It is our awareness of its reality of existence that strays. Awareness of mind allows you to look around as a witness, fully Present with what is now occurring. There is a joy of Being One with life in its aliveness; existing with all things in the moment of your awareness to them. You are in agreement with life's unfolding Presence and not in resistance to it by wanting more than what is. In gratitude and thanksgiving your mind is grounded for all that is in the now. This is our grounding Presence, our minds' right position. It is peace and joy in the Spirit as Jesus taught, peace and joy of Being One with life in the reality of its existence, this Present moment.

In all you do, do it in the glory or great praise of life in the Present moment. Be fully alive and Present to experience the joy of your vitality. You have the joy of Being One with life through a Present mind when you do things. It is taking pleasure in what you are doing, fully alert and alive in the moment. You are One with the doing, fully wrapped up in your awareness to it; as if time stands still, you are enjoying every detail of it. You take great delight in the awareness of the doing, as if you are totally lost in the activity of it. It is the Creative energy flow that takes momentum within you as you are grounded in the Presence of it. You are fully absorbed and content with the Oneness of Being Creative with the energy life flow within you. You are fully alive in your Being of Oneness with life itself!

SEEK LIFE'S PRESENCE

Seek the LORD** and his strength;
seek his presence continually**! *(Psalm 105:4)*

$\mathcal{A}$LL THINGS ARE ADDED TO YOUR AWARENESS IN A PRESENT STATE OF MIND.

Therefore do not be anxious, *saying, "What shall we eat?" or "What shall we drink?" or "What shall we wear?" For the Gentiles seek after all these things, and your heavenly Father knows that you need them all.* **But seek first the kingdom of God and his righteousness**, *and* **all these things will be added to you**. *(Matthew 6:31–33)*

$\mathcal{T}$HE SURRENDERD MIND (CHRIST) COMES INTO THE LIGHT OF AWARENESS OF LIFE'S PRESENCE, ITS OVERFLOWING VASTNESS AND GREATNESS IN AND THROUGH ALL.

The thief comes only to steal and kill and destroy. I came that they may have life and have it abundantly. *(John 10:10)*

$\mathcal{T}$HE GROUNDING OF A PRESENT MIND TO LIFE'S REALITY IS THROUGH THE CONTENTMENT OF BEING ONE WITH LIFE IN THE NOW; IT IS THE PEACE AND JOY OF BEING ONE WITH ALIVENESS.

Keep your life free from love of money, and **be content with what you have**, *for he has said,* **"I will never leave you nor forsake you."** *(Hebrews 13:5)*

$\mathcal{C}$OMING INTO A PRESENT STATE OF MIND THROUGH THE AWARENESS OF SPIRIT (BREATH).

For the kingdom of God is not a matter of eating and drinking, but **of righteousness**, **peace and joy in the** Holy **Spirit**. *(Romans 14:17)*

$\mathcal{D}$O EVERYTHING FULLY PRESENT OF MIND.

So, whether you eat or drink, or whatever you do, do all to **the glory of God**. *(1 Corinthians 10:31)*

Blessed be the God and Father of our Lord Jesus Christ, **who has blessed us in Christ** *with* **every spiritual blessing** *in the heavenly places ….* *(Ephesians 1:3)*

> **Oh, taste and see that the** Lord **is good**!
> > **Blessed is the man who takes refuge in him**!
> > *(Psalm 34:8)*

> **He is my steadfast love and my fortress**,
> > **my stronghold and my deliverer**,
> **my shield and he in whom I take refuge**,
> > *who subdues peoples under me. (Psalm 144:2)*

> *For you make him most* **blessed forever**;
> > *you make him* **glad with the joy of your**
> > **presence**. *(Psalm 21:6)*

> *Fear not,* **for I am with you**;
> > *be not dismayed, for I am your God;*
> **I will strengthen you**, **I will help you**,
> > **I will uphold you** *with my righteous right hand.*
> > *(Isaiah 41:10)*

May you be strengthened with all power, *according to his glorious might, for all* **endurance** *and* **patience** *with* **joy**. *(Colossians 1:11 RSV)*

> *""The Lord bless you*
> *and **keep you**;*
> *the Lord make his face **shine on you***
> *and be gracious to you;*
> *the Lord turn his face toward you*
> *and **give you peace**.""* *(Numbers 6:24–26 NIV)*

*Though you have not seen him, you love him. Though you do not now see him, **you believe in him** and **rejoice with joy that is inexpressible and filled with glory**. (1 Peter 1:8)*

Chapter 4.6

Walking in Newness of Life— You Are a New Creation

The New You

The Bible refers to having a new identity in Christ; that is, you are a new creation, for you have surrendered the false self, the ego. You are now born again of Spirit, or the mind's awareness to life's Presence in the now. The ego mind that creates an experience outside of life's Presence through its continual rationalizing and seeking has been put to death. You are free from the ego, the false self, and you are now a new creation, One with God Consciousness. You are One with the awareness of life itself. This is your newness—the mind's new awareness of the reality of life's Presence.

That which comes into the light of awareness is visible to the eyes and gives understanding to the mind's single eye. What remains in the dark is not visible but still hidden, for you are unaware of its existence. Therefore, bring all things to the light of your awareness, and you will see the truth or reality of what is before you.

Walking in the Light

In the light of our awareness, this Present and awake state of mind, we have Conscious clarity of what is: the true nature of life in its reality of existence. We have an open and alert mind to see all that is in front of us. Life's natural path, its unfolding of itself in the here and now, is visible to us. Nothing is hidden but fully Present in our keen awareness to it. Our minds are not cluttered or distracted but fully alert and poised.

You are in correct balance, in your right alignment with life's flow, this Conscious energy flow that is within and all around you. This is your awakened mind, the observing mind. Your mind has been renewed, for it is no longer the thinker, the seeker, but it has rested and become the observer. You are One with life; you are the witnessing Presence to life's unfolding existence. Your manner of walk in life is now new to you, reflecting all wisdom and understanding of the clarity of Consciousness, fully awake and alive in your Being of Oneness to it. You have the clear perception of life, the reality of it, through your observation of it. You are looking at the truth of what is, in full awareness.

You are not resisting life but have become One with it. You are in the river of life and you are flowing downstream with it. You are not struggling upstream but surrendering to its current and direction; this is the path of least resistance, you are going with the flow of life, surrendered to its ease and perfect timing. It is easy, it is peaceful, it is natural, and you are in perfect alignment with it through Being Present with its unfolding. This is your newness of life, walking in the light of awareness of it. Surrender to life's Presence!

Life is incredibly easy to live! Just be Present to it! Show up to life's incredible unfolding of itself!

And this newness of life? Walk in your awareness of it! Don't resist its unfolding, but be Present with it, in every moment!

Then you shall go forth in bold confidence, child. Let not fear reign in your heart but the Righteousness of My Spirit.

ℐRUST AND ENDURANCE

Stay the course; do not let your eyes fall away from Me, life's Presence at hand. If you are grounded in My strength, I will keep you, and you will endure all things. Have faith in life, trusting its existence, and remain in Me, your Conscious awareness.

You shall overcome all tests of the unconscious mind when you remain in a Present awareness of Me, life in the now. Trusting in Me fully, surrendering all to Me, will allow for your greatest success. I have already overcome so that you shall endure. So remain in Me, this Present moment of life!

Fear not, for I AM by your side, strengthening you to achieve all that you were meant to be. I AM your solid foundation, this firm Presence of life!

Surrender again when your mind has strayed from life's Presence, for I shall deliver you out of the depths of despair!

𝒜 MIND THAT IS GROUNDED IN TRUST

Trusting God, trusting life's Presence in the now, is letting go of the false self-awareness that was created outside of life's existence. Let not the ego overtake you, pulling you into an unconscious unawareness of life's Presence. The confusion and fear of not existing in reality shall reign in your heart. Come fully into the awareness of the Present moment! Trust the unfolding of life; become One with your inner Being of aliveness.

In surrender we become self-less and fear-less! Don't fear the worst, but trust life for the best!

Do not fear for the unknown. Leap out into the reality of what is!

Do not step out of the flow of life in your resistance to it, but remain Present in it. Make peace with its occurring, coming into an alignment with what is.

I will walk in this newness of life, fully planted in the Presence of Being, fully alive in the now of existence!

𝒥N CHRIST (DEATH OF SELF-AWARENESS) YOU ARE A NEW CREATION. YOU ARE NOW THE OBSERVER OR WITNESS TO LIFE'S PRESENCE IN THE NOW. THE NEW IS HERE, IT IS NOW.

Therefore, **if anyone is in Christ, the new creation has come**: *The old has gone, **the new is here**! (2 Corinthians 5:17)*

𝒯HE OLD FALSE SELF-AWARENESS IS GONE AND THE NEW OR THE TRUE IDENTITY OF WHO YOU ARE IS THE IMAGE OF YOUR CREATOR; GOD, THE CREATOR OF ALL LIFE. YOUR NEW IDENTITY IS GOD CONSCIOUSNESS.

*And have **put on the new self**, which is being **renewed in knowledge after the image of its creator**. (Colossians 3:10)*

𝒯HE EGO HAS DIED AND IS HIDDEN IN THE PRESENCE OF LIFE'S AWARENESS; A PRESENT STATE OF MIND.

For you have died, and your life is hidden *with Christ **in God**. (Colossians 3:3)*

*I **have been crucified with Christ**. It is **no longer I who live**, but Christ who lives in me. And the life I now live in the flesh I live by faith in the Son of God, who loved me and gave himself for me. (Galatians 2:20)*

𝒲ALKING IN THE NEWNESS OF LIFE IS THE MIND'S AWARENESS TO LIFE'S REALITY IN THE NOW; A PRESENT STATE OF MIND.

You make known to me the path of life;
    in your presence *there is fullness of joy;*
at your right hand are pleasures forevermore.
(Psalm 16:11)

We were buried therefore with him by *baptism into death*, in order that, just as Christ was raised from the dead by the glory of the Father, *we too might walk in newness of life*. (Romans 6:4)

$\mathcal{T}$HE RESURRECTION (RESTORED TO LIFE) IS THE MIND'S REBIRTH INTO THE AWARENESS OF CONSCIOUSNESS OR THE PRESENCE OF LIFE'S REALITY IN THE NOW.

Baptism, which corresponds to this, *now saves you*, not as a removal of dirt from the body but as an appeal *to God for a good conscience*, *through the resurrection* of Jesus Christ …. (1 Peter 3:21)

Again Jesus spoke to them, saying, "I am the light of the world. Whoever follows me will not walk in darkness, but will have the light of life." (John 8:12)

$\mathcal{W}$ALK OUT THE REALITY OF LIFE THROUGH YOUR MIND'S AWARENESS OF ITS PRESENCE.

*For at one time you were darkness, but now you are **light in the Lord. Walk as children of light**. (Ephesians 5:8)*

Chapter 4.7

One Collective Consciousness

We Are All One Collective Consciousness through a Present State of Mind

In your awareness to life's Presence you are One with the everlasting, eternal Creative Being that moves in and through you. It creates your very aliveness in this moment of your existence. We are all One with life, its power and motion, its ease and momentum. We have unity with it, as it freely flows within us, allowing our Being and motion of aliveness to exist. We are all of One body, as this same life force energy that is sustaining you is Present in all things living. We are the existence of the sustaining Presence of life itself, having our minds come into an awareness of its inner Being within us. We are all joined as One collective consciousness through a Present state of mind. We are all One, connected to each other and all things living, through this thread of creative life force energy. It is in all, and through all, sustaining all things in the now reality of existence.

$\mathcal{B}$ECOMING THE MIND OF CHRIST

Through your surrender of the ego's seeking mind, you hold every thought captive to its death. You have died to your false self-awareness, transcending the rationalizing and seeking mind to a stillness within. You have surrendered your mind's ways of seeking more beyond life's Presence, to an awareness of life's manifestation within you.

You now have become Consciously aware of what is, and this is your mind's renewal, having come to the observing or witnessing mind to life's Presence. You are now fully alive in this newness of being, aware to life's reality of existence. In your death, you have become the mind of Christ. Now you are the witnessing Presence, the observing mind to life in your awareness of it. Through the mind of Christ, you have transcended to the One mind of life's abiding Presence. You are awake, alert, and aware to life in the now, this existence of energy that is sustaining you.

$\mathcal{O}$NE THROUGH CONSCIOUS AWARENESS OF LIFE'S PRESENCE

The mind that has aligned itself with the ego, the false self-awareness, has sought life beyond its Present existence. It is an illusion created by the mind, an experience of death, for no life exists beyond its reality of Presence. Your surrender of the false self-awareness brings you into the awareness of life's Presence. You are now One with life's reality of existence: One with God, the Spirit, the life flow energy within. You are One mind through the Conscious Presence of life within.

We are all *One* in Presence of mind, *One* Conscious awareness to Being fully Present. We are all *One* in God through a Present state of mind.

$\mathcal{S}$EEKING THE MIND OF GOD

Do not be distracted by the ego, yet hide your false self-awareness and its seeking mind. Look not to the world and all its luring desires, for it leads you away from My Presence, life's reality. Come to a place of complete stillness, and wait for Me there. Become quiet in your thoughts, surrendering to this quiet peaceful moment we have together.

In your reverence to Me, your Conscious awareness to My abiding Presence, you must quiet your mind to draw near to Me. Wait patiently as if you are to hear something. And when you have been still and quiet for some time, I will come to you! I will reveal Myself to you! You will know it is I, through your Conscious awareness of My Presence. Immediately, you are consumed with

My peace, because your mind has rested. It no longer seeks anything but has rested in this moment of stillness, this moment of life's Presence. Remain here for a while, in this Present moment, and I will refresh your soul. Do not let the world distract you in all you have to do. But remain here with My Presence, and I shall give you rest and restore you. You shall feel My Spirit overtake you! You shall be aware of My Being flowing through you, My life energy.

In your surrender to Me, this moment of your awareness to life in the now, we are One. One body, One mind, One Spirit. Shall you lend an ear to Me, child? Surrender to the mind of awareness, the mind of witnessing! And I shall speak to you when you are quietly waiting, for My intuitive thoughts shall arise within you! I shall overtake your mind, and My wisdom and understanding will begin to flow to you in inspired thoughts. Like a living fountain, My thoughts will spring up within you, wisdom and understanding will flow into your mind through your Conscious awareness.

It is here that you will know that I, the Living God, AM a God of hosts! I shall dwell in you, as you are My vessel to host My Spirit, the life force energy within. Embrace Me in this moment of your surrender, as I enter your awareness! And we become One, having One mind through Conscious awareness. Become fully alive in Me, child! Surrender to Being One with life, found in this moment of Being fully Present in your mind! Stay awake and Present, having your mind set upon Me, for I have much to tell you!

Oh, how alive You are within Me! How wonderful it is to be free of the self and to become *One* with You! I have entered life, Eternal Presence, in this moment of Being fully aware to life as it is. For, in this moment of Presence, my mind's place of rest and stillness, I need nothing, for I have You!

This is your very reward, your crown of life's Presence! You have entered the gate through the gatekeeper; he who has died to his mind's self-awareness has come back to the awareness of life itself!

He who has denied his mind's seeking beyond life in the now, has become alive in the Presence of Being One with life! This is the key to Heaven, that which unlocks the gate to enter the City! You have surrendered the false self-awareness, the death experience, and have become fully aware of life's Present existence found in the now of reality.

Do not deny the Presence of life, the now reality of its existence. For life is only found in this moment of Being Present to it! Nothing exists beyond this moment, and your ego has created a delusion, a distraction of the mind to go beyond the now of Being One with life.

$\mathcal{O}$NE MIND

Through our Conscious awareness to life's Presence within, we are One with God. We are One with wisdom, understanding, the Conscious clarity of what is. We are fully aware of life in this moment of reality, its Present existence. We are One with life, the Creator of all things living. Just as Jesus declared, *I and the Father are One*, we too become One with the Father of all Creation, the life force energy within, through our minds' awareness of its abiding Presence.

Those who have sacrificed themselves for Me have overcome the world.

Crucify the self-awareness, the false self, as Jesus did. Overcome the world's distractions, all that your ego seeks beyond My Presence, and you shall become One with Me. You shall embrace life in your awareness of it, this Present moment of Being One with it.

147

$\mathcal{G}$OD, THE LIFE FORCE ENERGY, IS ONE.

Hear, O Israel: **The Lord our God, the Lord is one.** *(Deuteronomy 6:4)*

There is one body and **one Spirit**—*just as you were called to the one hope that belongs to your call—***one Lord**, **one faith, one baptism**, **one God and Father of all**, **who is over all** *and* **through all and in all**. *(Ephesians 4:4–6)*

$\mathcal{J}$ESUS, LIVING IN A PRESENT STATE OF MIND (I AM IN THE FATHER) WITH THE AWARENESS THAT THE FATHER OF ALL CREATION (LIFE FORCE ENERGY) IS IN HIM (THE FATHER IS IN ME).

$\mathcal{T}$HE PRESENT STATE OF MIND (THE MIND THAT DWELLS IN THE NOW) ALLOWS GOD TO MANIFEST (HIS WORKS).

Jesus said to him, "Have I been with you so long, and you still do not know me, Philip? **Whoever has seen me has seen the Father**. *How can you say, 'Show us the Father'? Do you not believe that* **I am in the Father** *and* **the Father is in me**? *The words that I say to you I do not speak on my own authority,* **but the Father who dwells in me does his works**." *(John 14:9–10)*

On that day you will realize **that I am in my Father**, *and* **you are in me**, *and* **I am in you**. *(John 14:20 NIV)*

I and the Father are one. *(John 10:30)*

$\mathcal{W}$E ARE ALL ONE HAVING ALIGNED OUR MINDS TO A PRESENT STATE OF AWARENESS TO LIFE'S EXISTENCE.

Complete my joy by **being of the same mind**, *having the same love,* **being in full accord and of one mind**. *(Philippians 2:2)*

But he who is joined to the Lord becomes one spirit with him. *(1 Corinthians 6:17)*

Chapter 4.8

The Voice of God—Inspired Thoughts through the Power of Presence

Inspiration Arising from a Conscious Present State of Mind

Through a Present state of mind you are fully open and connected to the infinite source of all life, the unlimited Being of all intelligence, the One collective Conscious Presence. And through your clarity of Consciousness, your alert and awakened mind, inspired thoughts and ideas arise that begin to form understanding. There is reflection of insight, and wisdom flows freely. You are caught up in Divine intelligence with unlimited comprehension, through a mind that is free and open to allow the free flowing Divine inspiration to come through. There is wisdom and a sense of knowing to what is, through a mind that is clear and awake. You are fully connected to Conscious awareness, One with Infinite intelligence, the source and Creator of all life.

A Present state of mind through its awareness is able to receive the internal discourse, the inner communication, with the all-knowing Infinite source of wisdom. And out of your mind's stillness, you will hear an inner voice that will give you counsel and direction. You are internally connected to this Infinite source of all knowledge, this free flowing life force energy that is manifesting within you in the now of life's reality, this Present moment.

And if you struggle, if you lose your identity and fall out of My Presence, into the darkness of the unaware mind, I, Infinite intelligence, will speak to you, pulling you out of the darkness and back into My light of awareness. I shall rescue you from the depth of despair, piercing your Consciousness. You shall hear My voice. And My words spoken to you will quicken you and strengthen you! I will carry you out of your destruction and into My Presence of salvation. You will suffer no more, for in your mind's right standing, you are fully Present with Me! It is I, life's reality!

The words of God are of great mystery and revelation! Listen, all who have an ear! Become the observing and listening mind for the voice of God that speaks!

A word is just a word until one is given understanding of it. Then it becomes a revelation!

𝒯REE OF LIFE

Be Present of mind, in Oneness with Me. For I will give you all wisdom and understanding, and then you will hear My words in which to speak. They shall rise up within you! I shall inspire you with My great wisdom and understanding. For I have created you all to be My prophets and to hear My voice. In the moment of your Present and alert mind, you shall hear, and I shall inspire you with great motivation. I shall give you the answers that you seek to know. Shall you be still and quiet within your mind so that you can hear them? Listen intuitively, for I speak. Quiet your mind, surrender your will to rationalize, and I will come upon you with great wisdom. What are you seeking? I shall tell you, look, there it is! What are you trying to resolve? I shall reveal this to you! Your clarity of mind only exists in My Presence. Listen for My voice, child; be still! I AM your breath of inspiration, your clarity of discernment and direction; I AM your wisdom and source of all knowledge! For I AM the tree called life, and you are My branch, you are the extension of all that I AM.

𝒯HE VOICE OF GOD

Oh, how much better it is to eat the fruit of the Tree of Life than to suffer and perish in your mental darkness. Those who continue to fall from My Presence in their mind's seeking beyond life's existence are plunged into their unawareness of what truly is. Yet they do not know that they have left the Presence of My Being within them. They have no awareness of life's existence, found only in this Present moment. They have fallen into the state of unawareness of Me, My life force energy. They have not chosen to come into the light of awareness to what is, My Present existence. Their minds have deceived them, for they think life is beyond this Present moment of time. And in all their seeking for more, they have been absent to life themselves. They have stepped out into their death, the nonexistence of life's reality.

Yet I shall call out to them! Yes, I wish to end their suffering in this moment. I shall pierce their Consciousness and make them aware of Being Present in their mind. I shall deliver them from death and bring them into the light of awareness of life's existence! Yes, I would break the chains of suffering that they find bound to their necks. I will quicken them this instant and bring them back to the awareness of life!

$\mathcal{T}$HE VOICE WITHIN

Come, child, let Me whisper in your ear. Let Me tell you secrets that you have not known, that have not been revealed since the beginning of time. Yes, I AM life, and I AM heard through your awareness of My Presence within. You know My voice, for you have stood at My footstool eager to hear a word of clarity. I have strengthened you in your thoughts and understanding. I shall uphold you through all your trials when you are fully Present in Me! Yes, I AM the existence of life, and I shall keep you in this Present moment of My existence. The Heavens shall reveal My Glory to you, in your awareness of Me, My Spirit, the life force energy that is sustaining you! It shall overcome you in your temple, through your awareness of Me. The Presence of My life force energy shall be upon you, for no other can manifest within you, as no other has formed you. I have made you with every thread of My Being interwoven within you. I shall be made known in your awareness of Me, for you are a child of My life force energy. I give you Being and aliveness in this moment of awareness. And as you *know Me, this life force within, I also know you. You have heard My voice that pierced your Consciousness, fully awakening you to what is. My thoughts of understanding are freely given in your awareness of My Presence! Come seek Me, life in this Present moment! Come listen to My voice, and I shall open your mind to great wisdom. I shall give you My thoughts, and fill your mind with great understanding! Come, child, there is much to share with you!*

$\mathcal{T}$HE VOICE OF SALVATION

Behold! There is a king, a Mighty One who saves. You hear Him, and you know Him, for He is within you, abiding in your innermost Being, your Conscious awareness. He is above all your thoughts and above all your ways. So rise above your thoughts to the mind's stillness, and you shall find Him. You shall know His voice, words that pierce your Conscious awareness. He will call you out of the darkness, the imprisoned mind that exists outside the Presence of life in this moment. There is a silent whisper that you must quiet your self to hear. And in the light of your awareness through your observing mind, you shall hear the voice of God speak.

$\mathcal{I}$N THE LIGHT OF MY AWARENESS, I HEAR YOU

You are my shelter in the storms of life. You lift me up to Your Presence. Your word is spoken to me in the dead of night. Oh, how my soul has waited for Your voice! And like a thief in the night, without any warning, You come! You speak to me, and I know You are within me. Your voice of encouragement lifts me out of the depths of darkness, my deepest despair! You have made Yourself known to me! You shelter me in the house of my God! Your voice is My salvation! You have pulled me out of the torment of my mind. I hear Your voice, and I believe in Your salvation, because it is Your voice that speaks! Joy and gladness have filled my heart because You are Present, and I hear You!

$\mathcal{A}$ND THE WORD OF THE LORD CAME

Call out to Me in your stillness, and I will deliver you. I will take you out of the darkness, your unawareness of Me; for you have been led astray from My Presence of life. In your darkest hour, I AM here. I AM your shelter and protector. You are a slave no more to the mind's thoughts, yet have come into the light of awareness, in your witnessing of My Presence. I shall raise you up in your awareness and restore you to your right standing, your Presence of mind. I shall make you whole and complete in your Consciousness, your awareness to what is, life in this very Present moment.

Do not be afraid, and do not worry, for that is a mind that has left My Presence of life in the now. Trust in Me, for I AM your salvation and deliverer, I AM your awareness to life's Present moment, its reality of existence. Remain in Me, this light of awareness to life found in your mind's Presence to it.

My thoughts are above your thoughts—enter into the mind of Conscious awareness.

Surrender your self-awareness, rising above your thoughts. Wait in silence as the observing witness to listen, to hear the thoughts of God!

Rise above the thinking mind to find the Present mind of Conscious awareness, for you are now the witnessing or observing mind to God's wisdom and understanding!

The wisdom that comes from God strikes you with great profoundness. In awe, you are transformed in your awareness of the truth, your identity, and Oneness with life itself!

$\mathcal{T}$HE WORD OF GOD DELIVERS

The heavens will open, and My word shall come forth. It shall go out and deliver a message entering through your light of awareness. For all will become weary, and hunger for My direction. All will struggle with fears and unknowns, and they shall call out to Me, and My words shall deliver them. Indeed, My word shall bring them overwhelming peace, for they have been brought into the awareness of My Presence, and they shall shout with joy. For their God has rescued them, delivering their minds from death, their unawareness to My existence. And in their mental awareness, fully Present mind, they will know My words, and they shall know My voice.

I shall speak to those who surrender to Me, life in this Present moment of their awareness! And I will deliver them! Yes, I will deliver them from the mental darkness and bring them to the full awareness of life, found only in a Present mind. They will hear My voice! Indeed, My word shall go out to the earth, and it shall rest on the hearts that seek Me! My word will do all that I have sent it out to do!

Be of a Present mind, alert and aware to life in this moment! It is here in this Present state of mind that Conscious clarity, life's wisdom, will flow through you.

It is Christ, your death and surrender of the mind's false self-awareness, that allows you to become the observing witness to the emerging Presence of life within.

Become awakened to the word of God who speaks to your inner Being of aliveness, found only in a Present state of mind.

The Voice of the False Self Leads Your Mind Astray

The mind that has fallen from its right standing position, its Conscious clarity of Oneness with life in this Present moment, is one of a false self-awareness. There is a constant run-on dialogue within the mind that continues to rationalize and give explanation of all things, avoiding the truth of what is. There is an internal conflict, a struggle to be right, an interference to what is in this moment of life's reality; it is a fallacy of the mind. It is the argumentative thought flow within, a mind that fails to quiet itself. It is the mind that continues to affirm, deny, and judge by reason of thoughts; it is the argumentative discourse within. It is the mind's automatic and continual thought processes of desires, interests, and memories with little or no introspection. The mind is continually trapped in its never-ending run-on dialogue of thoughts. It has not reached a point of reprieve, a moment of Conscious awareness to clarity of what is. It is not a mind that is clear in its alertness and wakeful state. There is no capacity to recognize inspired thought for the mind has not quieted itself long enough to allow Conscious awareness to come through. Your mind is lost, through its unawareness, from the Presence of life, the reality of its existence in the here and now.

$\mathcal{G}$OD IS INFINITE INTELLIGENCE; THE SOURCE OF ALL WISDOM AND UNDERSTANDING.

In the beginning was the Word, and *the Word was with God,* and *the Word was God*. *(John 1:1)*

$\mathcal{T}$HE ARISING AWARENESS OF INTUITION; THE INSPIRED THOUGHTS AND IDEAS THAT GIVE US GUIDANCE AND WORDS TO SPEAK.

The Beginning of Knowledge
The proverbs of Solomon, son of David, king of Israel:

> *To know wisdom and instruction*,
>   *to understand words of insight*,
> to *receive instruction* in wise dealing,
>   in *righteousness*, justice, and equity;
> to give prudence to the simple,
>   *knowledge and discretion* to the youth—
> Let the wise *hear* and *increase in learning*,
>   and the one who understands *obtain guidance*.
>   *(Proverbs 1:1–5)*

Now the word of the LORD *came to me*, saying,

> "Before I formed you in the womb I knew you,
> and before you were born I consecrated you;
> *I appointed you a prophet to the nations*."
>   *(Jeremiah 1:4–5)*

For no prophecy was ever produced by the will of man, but *men spoke from God as they were carried along by the Holy Spirit*. *(2 Peter 1:21)*

For the Holy Spirit will teach you in that very hour what you ought to say. *(Luke 12:12)*

For I will give you a mouth and wisdom, *which none of your adversaries will be able to withstand or contradict. (Luke 21:15)*

𝒴OU HAVE FORSAKEN YOUR (EGO) WAYS AND THOUGHTS AND HAVE RISEN ABOVE THEM AND RETURNED TO THE WITNESSING, THE OBSERVING, THE LISTENING MIND OF CONSCIOUS AWARENESS.

"**Let the wicked forsake their ways**
    and the unrighteous their thoughts.
Let them turn to the Lord,
    and he will have mercy on them,
and to our God,
    for he will freely pardon.
For my thoughts are not your thoughts,
    neither are your ways my ways,"
    declares the Lord.
"As **the heavens are higher** *than the earth,*
    so are **my ways higher** *than your ways*
    and my thoughts *than your thoughts."*
    (Isaiah 55:7–9 NIV)

And if you faithfully obey the voice of the Lord *your God*, *being careful to do all his commandments that I command you today, the* Lord *your God will set you high above* all the nations of the earth. And all these blessings shall come upon you and overtake you,* **if you obey the voice of the** Lord **your God**. *(Deuteronomy 28:1–2)*

𝒲ITHOUT THE MIND'S EYE OF AWARENESS, THE LISTENING MIND, YOU FAIL TO UNDERSTAND WHAT GOD HAS PREPARED FOR YOU IN THIS LIFE.

But, as it is written,

> *"**What no eye has seen**, **nor ear heard**,*
>   *nor the heart of man imagined,*
> *what God has prepared for those who*
>   *love him"*—

$\mathcal{G}$OD REVEALS HIS PLANS FREELY TO THE MIND THAT IS PRESENT IN THE NOW. YOU BECOME ONE WITH THE SOURCE OF ALL INFINITE WISDOM AND KNOWLEDGE.

*these things God has revealed to us through the Spirit. For the Spirit searches everything, even the depths of God. For who knows a person's thoughts except the spirit of that person, which is in him? So also **no one comprehends the thoughts of God except the Spirit of God. Now we have received** not the spirit of the world, but **the Spirit who is from God, that we might understand the things freely given us by God**. And we impart this in words not taught by human wisdom but **taught by the Spirit**, interpreting spiritual truths to those who are spiritual. (1 Corinthians 2:9–13)*

$\mathcal{G}$OD'S KNOWLEDGE CANNOT BE ATTAINED THROUGH THE RATIONALIZING MIND BUT THROUGH THE MIND OF SURRENDER TO RISE ABOVE (HIGH).

> *Such knowledge is too wonderful for me;*
>   *it is high; I cannot attain it.*
> *Where shall I go from your Spirit?*
>   *Or where shall I flee from your presence?*
> *If I ascend to heaven, you are there!*
>   *If I make my bed in Sheol, you are there. (Psalm 139:6–8)*

$\mathcal{I}$NSPIRED WISDOM AND UNDERSTANDING FLOWS AS GOD'S THOUGHTS ENTER INTO YOUR MIND'S AWARENESS.

How precious to me are your thoughts, O God!
How vast is the sum of them!
If I would count them, they are more than the sand.
I awake, and I am still with you. *(Psalm 139:17–18)*

You have multiplied, O Lord my God,
your wondrous deeds and **your thoughts
toward us**;
none can compare with you!
**I will proclaim and tell of them,
yet they are more than can be told**.
(Psalm 40:5)

*Y*OU HAVE BECOME THE LISTENING MIND (EAR) TO THE VOICE OF GOD.

**Let me hear what God the Lord will speak,
for he will speak peace to his people**,
to his saints; but let them not turn back to folly.
(Psalm 85:8)

To him the gatekeeper opens. **The sheep hear his voice**, and **he calls his own sheep by name and leads them out**. When he has brought out all his own, he goes before them, and **the sheep follow him**, **for they know his voice**. A stranger they will not follow, but they will flee from him, for they do not know the voice of strangers. *(John 10:3–5)*

My sheep **hear my voice**, **and I know them**, and they follow me. *(John 10:27)*

But he answered, "It is written,

> "'Man shall not live by bread alone,
>   but **by every word that comes from the mouth
>   of God**.'" *(Matthew 4:4)*

Behold, I stand at the door and knock. **If anyone hears my voice** *and opens the door,* **I will come in to him and eat with him, and he with me**. *(Revelation 3:20)*

Then the LORD **called Samuel**, *and he said, "Here I am!" and ran to Eli and said, "Here I am, for you called me." But he said, "I did not call; lie down again." So he went and lay down.*

  And the LORD ***called again**, "Samuel!" and Samuel arose and went to Eli and said, "Here I am, for you called me." But he said, "I did not call, my son; lie down again."* **Now Samuel did not yet know the** LORD**, and the word of the** LORD **had not yet been revealed to him.**

  And the LORD **called Samuel again the third time**. *And he arose and went to Eli and said, "Here I am, for you called me."* **Then Eli perceived that the** LORD **was calling the boy**. *Therefore Eli said to Samuel,* **"Go, lie down, and if he calls you, you shall say, 'Speak,** LORD**, for your servant hears.'"** *So Samuel went and lay down in his place. (1 Samuel 3:4–9)*

𝒴OU WILL KNOW THE VOICE OF CLARITY IN THE STILL MIND, THE LISTENING MIND OF AWARENESS.

For the word of God is living and active, *sharper than any two-edged sword,* **piercing** *to the division of soul and of spirit, of joints and of marrow, and* **discerning the thoughts** *and intentions of the heart. (Hebrews 4:12)*

> **On the day I called**, **you answered me**;
>   **my strength of soul you increased**.[
> *All the kings of the earth shall give you thanks, O* LORD,
>   **for they have heard the words of your mouth**,

and they shall sing of **the ways of the L**ORD,
>for great is the glory of the LORD. *(Psalm 138:3–5)*

He sent out his word and healed them,
>and **delivered them from their destruction.**
>*(Psalm 107:20)*

Ascribe to the LORD, *O heavenly beings,*
>**ascribe to the L**ORD *glory and strength.*
Ascribe to the LORD *the glory due his name;*
>*worship the* LORD *in the splendor of holiness.*
The voice of the LORD *is over the waters;*
>*the God of glory thunders,*
>*the* LORD, *over many waters.*
The voice of the LORD **is powerful**;
>*the voice of the* LORD *is full of majesty.*
The voice of the LORD **breaks the cedars**;
>*the* LORD *breaks the cedars of Lebanon.*
>*(Psalm 29:1–5)*

So shall my word be that goes out from my mouth;
>*it shall not return to me empty,*
but **it shall accomplish that which I purpose,**
>*and* **shall succeed in the thing for which I sent**
>**it**. *(Isaiah 55:11)*

Chapter 4.9

A New Purpose—Your Inherited
Power and Intent

The Purpose and Plan of Life's Existence Has Already Been Determined

You have now aligned your mind with the Present moment reality of life's existence by becoming the observing or the witnessing mind to life's now occurring in this time of reality. You see life as it is unfolding right in front of you. You are not in a mental place of resistance to life's occurring in the now, but you are One with it. You are not stumbling in the dark of unawareness to life in the now, but you are in the light of awareness of its existence. You see things quite clearly, how they are meant to be. There is no confusion of what is but peace in knowing the truth of reality. You are in your mind's right position, its right standing, its perfect alignment with life in your witnessing of it. You have come to this place of reality, and you are noticing its energy flow, its ease of motion, its grace, as you observe this Present state of mind, this place called life. You have been born again, newly planted within the mind's Present state, and have been crowned with the gift of life's Presence.

You are now back on track with life's occurring, fully prepared, fully alert, and awake to your surroundings. Your mind is not cluttered with rationalizing thought but it is clear, sharp, and ready to listen intuitively. And in this fully Conscious clarity of mind, wisdom and understanding begin to flow to you. Things are really coming together for you; they make sense, and you are gaining understanding of all aspects of this place called life that you have now stepped into. You are One with the Divine Intelligence, and your mind begins to receive this wonderful flow of wisdom and understanding of life through the clarity of the Present mind. You see life in your awareness of it, its reality of the here and now existence.

Out of the quiet mind, the observing awareness to what is, inspired thoughts arise from within to your Present mind's Conscious awareness: a flow of intuitive conversation, an internal dialogue. You are the listener and the observer, and life is revealing incredible insight through its intuitive design. Your purpose and your existence and Oneness with life in this here and now of reality are emerging within your Consciousness. You gain clarity through your awareness and understanding of who you really are. New desires begin to form in you with purposeful intent, a burning and longing to carry out what you were meant to do through your Presence with life. You have been given new purpose and desires, for you are One with the creative energy within. Christ is seated at the right hand of God – your mind in its present state of awareness freely accesses the right hemisphere of the brain because you have now let go of the rationalizing, linear thinking. The right hemisphere is the intuitive and creative side of your brain which allows you to tap into your imagination (we are made in His image) using visualization. You are now positioned or seated on high, the highest level of your brains functioning to allow the Divine Creator within you to flow freely.

Your sense of intuitive knowing now becomes your will, the commitment to live out life's Present existence through you. You are on purpose, having been assigned your position with life, firm in your action, steady and resolute to complete your task. You have fortitude, the power to complete your purpose, because life in its unfolding is One with you. Life, in your Oneness with it, supports and guides you along your journey. You will be given clear direction to go this way or that, and life's unfolding Presence will open doors to show you the way. You have now set out with life's abiding Presence by your side, equipped with a new purpose, a new mission to complete. And as you remain in the Present following along the path of life's unfolding journey, you continue to have a mind that is *listening* intuitively for the counsel and direction being given.

The path of life before you will light up in your awareness of it; then you just have to walk in it. Life will naturally unfold itself as you begin to walk forward in it. You are walking out the will of life, having become One with it in your awareness of its existence; you are following life's Divine purpose and plan, the why of your creation.

Life has already been set out for you; don't resist its unfolding. It all shall appear within your awareness of its existence, right before your very eyes. Wake up, sleeper, and look about you. Do you not see? Are you not Present within your mind to see life's reality? Listen, quiet your mind, and I shall tell you of the plan ahead for your journey; yes, I shall give you the direction of where to go.

Walk humbly before Me, surrendering your false awareness, and I will show you the only way that was ever intended for you to travel. Do not resist the unfolding of life, for within it lies your prosperity.

*Y*OUR HIDDEN PURPOSE

The secrets of life's existence are locked and hidden within you, only revealed to those who reverence Me. Come find Me, the Presence of life, through your Conscious awareness in this moment of reality. It is here you will know your identity, your Oneness with Me, your purposeful driven intent, the very reason why I created you! Meditate upon the Presence of just Being, and through your solitude and stillness of mind I will come to you! Through your Present state of mind of Being One in aliveness, My awareness shall emerge within you.

Now continue to be My observer, be the witnessing mind, and lend your ear to Me, for I have much to reveal to you!

I shall speak truths to you! I shall reveal to you the secret of your life's journey. Become One with My Spirit, life in the now through your mind, which is fully aware. I shall await here until you become aware of My emerging Presence within! Come sit at My footstool, and call out to Me! Seek Me earnestly, and I will pour wisdom over you. I will flood your gates with knowledge of life and purpose! Yes, give heed to Me, and I will come dine with you! I will open your mind through your Conscious awareness to life in this Present moment; I shall make Myself known to you.

I shall give you a purpose. Look to Me for direction, and you will succeed gracefully.

ⅅURPOSEFUL INTENT

It is here that you shall not stumble, but walk boldly in the direction I give you. Your mind will be filled with the assurance and confidence of the direction that has been given. I will wash away all your doubts and fears when you have surrendered to this Present moment in awareness of Me. In this newness of life, found in the very Presence of Being, I will give you the desire, My purpose and plan, placed upon your heart. And in your moment of surrender to the unfolding of life as it is, in the Being One with Me in the Presence of your mind, life will begin to unfold as it was meant to. Trust Me for these things, for I know the plans I have for you. I am the gentle breeze that comes in the early morning, so have your mind alert and ready, and be Present for My coming!

I dwell in the hearts of many who wait upon My arrival. Sit upon My doorstep, and be patient in your stillness, and then I shall whisper My thoughts, My direction to you.

Through My doors that are opened, you shall face no resistance. You will know exactly where to go. Just walk in life's natural path of unfolding, and I, life's existence, will light your way! I shall fill your mind with My thoughts, and you will gain understanding of My guidance and instruction for you!

You are One with the life flow energy, One with its ease and grace. You are going with the flow of life, this current of purposeful power and intent. This Oneness and acceptance of life is your ability to walk with it.

Let go of the false self to be aware of life's manifesting Presence within. Come into your mind's alignment, your agreement, with its existence. Do not resist the path of life, but continue in the flow of its now occurring.

There is never a struggle with life in your surrender to its unfolding. You are One with it, its unfolding purpose and intent.

ONE MIND AND ONE PURPOSE WITH LIFE

You are a reflection of life in your observing witness to it. You have not resisted life, yet you have surrendered to its natural unfolding of itself, becoming One with life in a Present state of mind. You have completely surrendered to the flow of life, its predetermined plan, its existence and reality of all that is.

In a fully wakeful mind, you are alert at all times to life's plan, to its natural flow. You are now walking in the Spirit, fully alive in every moment to your awareness of it. You need not step out of the Present moment, for no life exists beyond its reality. You are now, in this moment, fully alive and appreciative of the life force that is flowing through you. This energy of Being and aliveness is the flow of Spirit, the flow of life, within you. You live each moment in the now, never stepping outside of this mental state of Being Present with it. In your alert mind, this clarity of Consciousness, the will of life (God) is manifested through you. In this alert mind, new desires will come into your awareness: a vision, a purpose, and a plan. This is the will of life's existence flowing through you, for you have denied your false self-awareness to allow the greater awareness of life's plan to unfold through you.

I change the minds and hearts of those who love and seek Me, who hunger for more of life's Presence, and who are searching for their true purpose.

$\mathcal{M}$Y DESIRES

My self-focused desires are being washed away in the very Presence of life itself. For I, this false ego, this false created identity, have died. In this Present moment of awareness, I lack no good thing for all of life's existence is here with me. The abundant life Presence has come into my awareness of this moment, and I am alive in my Being of Oneness with it. I am consumed by life, completely aware of its abiding Presence within. I have conformed to Christ, sacrificing the false self-awareness that seeks all beyond the Presence of life's existence. I become One with the Presence of life itself, and in Him I am fulfilled, for I need nothing of this world beyond this moment of existence. When I become self-focused, the world appeals to me. I have this to do and that, all of which lures me away from Being Present with life. Yet I shall remain in Him, this Present moment of life, surrendering the false reality, the illusion of what is. Life's existence and purpose through me are greater. My desires and intent lie within life's reality itself!

I have been shown the way to the everlasting existing life, this Present moment of existence. It is through my Conscious awareness that I am Present, knowing the reality of life's occurring in the now. I've been filled with immeasurable life flow, its purposeful intent and knowing, the burning desire to see its fulfillment within. I shall only walk in the way of life's natural unfolding. I shall go this way and that, just as life instructs. I am on purpose, with intent and fortitude. I am strong in my determination, for my instructions are clear; I have clarity in this Conscious awareness of life's Presence.

Nothing of true worth in life can be achieved without an internal sense of driven purpose, a clear vision of what can be done, and a burning desire to see it achieved.

The drawing of God is calling you. It is a deep and burning desire to fulfill His purpose through you.

In My Presence, My desires overcome you. Your desires have fallen away.

$\mathcal{C}$ALLING

I have no peace about where I am in this life, dear Lord. I feel uprooted and stirred within my soul. I have a longing to move from this place. But where shall I go? What shall I do? Surely, O Lord, You have the plans set into place. As surely as the sun rises by day and sets by night, Your will shall be done. O Lord, work in me, Your servant! Stir Your Presence within me. Make Yourself known to me. Become One with me. And I shall surely hear Your voice! You will reveal your plans to me. Your servant waits for You with a listening ear!

Fear not, child, for I have made the way. You now know the path you shall take, for My will has been shown to you. Have I not told you these things? Have I not made Myself known to you in the depths of your soul, within your Consciousness? It is I, your God who speaks, who calls you forward. Walk in the way that I have revealed. Hold tight to My vision. Do not abandon Me, but hold fast to My Presence, and we shall accomplish great things together!

$\mathcal{I}$N BETWEEN

I lie in between heaven and earth. Full of hope and despair, I am left to walk this path, for my knowledge gained from You, O Lord, does not allow me to go fully back to this world. I now have understanding. I must stay in this position with hope of more understanding to move forward.

What I know now gives no reason to go back to the world in which I lived. The world's ways are beneath me. I have no desire to befriend it or to nurture it. All I desire is to seek Your Presence. I cannot explain these desires; they are like an addiction that You have placed within me. I am caught up. I am enthralled by the sheer magic of Your hold on me. "Why am I here?" I question. Without such purpose, I am nothing. I cannot go back to the world in which I was born. I cannot fully live in it because I desire more; I desire more of You, the existence of life's reality! The burning desire to be more and to do more is within me. Oh, how I long to get to that Present existence, but I am in between, not fully there.

Take hold of me, O Lord! Bring me near to Your Presence. Reveal to me the truth of the longings You have placed within my heart! Yes, reveal to me Your will! Reveal to me that burning desire I cannot put out! Come near me, O God, and reveal Your mighty plans to me. Quench this thirst I have to be One with You! Let me be fully caught up in Your Presence, forsaking the world! I await You at your footstool in between heaven and earth!

$\mathcal{T}$HE FORK IN THE ROAD

Shall you not lay down your life for Me? Shall you not gain the very Presence of life, its true existence, in exchange for death, this unreality of life in which you remain? There is no greater love than this: that a man shall lay down his own life for another. As I have loved you, My life was given for your sake. And now, for your sake, you must lay down your life for Me. For whoever loves his life shall lose it, and whoever hates his life for the sake of Me shall gain it. You have been called out of the darkness into the great light of awareness, to follow life. In all your existence, you have been following your false self-desires, and they have led you away from life's true Presence, your purpose and great plan. Now I have called you, child, out of the darkness, into the light of awareness of what is unfolding.

So there lies the fork in the road. The road before you is where you shall reside in existence. You can gain life in the now, this Present moment, or remain in your darkness of the unawareness to its abiding Presence within and all around you. You stand at the crossroads, and the choice is yours, child. Come into the light of awareness to all that is! Remain Present, fully alive in your Oneness with life's unfolding. It is here I shall reveal your true purpose, why I, the life force energy and Divine intelligence, have created you into Being! Come, listen to what I shall reveal. Sit quietly, and I shall speak to you. I shall reveal the incredible journey you will follow!

Come back to humble beginnings. This is the start of something great!

ℱALLING FROM LIFE'S PURPOSE

There is conflict when I fall from my purpose, when I fall out of the Presence of life, in my unawareness of it. There is struggle, strife, and pain when I stray from this moment of life's existence. If I live in the mind's continual seeking for more and not in the stillness and acceptance of what is, I lose my connection with life's reality! I have lost my ability to walk out my purpose and life's great plan of revealing it! I shall come back to my awareness of life in this moment. I shall wait for my instruction with a listening mind. I will align myself with life, and it will reveal to me the path in which I shall go; it will direct me in all the ways.

𝒯HE UNFOLDING PLAN

Your eagerness surpasses My timing, and so you fear the unknown. Your eagerness has led you to stray from the Present moment of life. I AM with you, upon you in Spirit. I will surely make Myself known to you in these directions. Have patience, child, in a moment of Presence, while these things come into your awareness. I will keep you on the path. Your Father has not left you. Never shall I leave you nor forsake you. You are not led aimlessly, wandering about. Have patience in your mind's stillness for My guidance and direction. Trust Me, for this shall come.

$\mathcal{T}$HE WAY YOU SHALL GO

The door will be open for you. Do not push open the doors that I have closed; that is not My will for you. There is no resistance in My will. Seek My Presence within your mind. My thoughts will become your thoughts. I will speak to your heart, your Consciousness. Do not go against My laws, for they have already been set in place, and they govern all things.

$\mathcal{T}$HE FLOW OF THE RIVER OF LIFE

The false self-seeking is not your purpose, for you, *the false self*, have died. And in the surrender of the ego, you have become One with God, One with the Being of life, One with the Creator of all existence. You have died, and this earthly vessel manifests the living Spirit of God, manifesting life in the now of reality, this space and time of existence. And in the ego's death, you have surrendered to a Present state of mind, no longer seeking for more, but it is still in its witnessing to what is now occurring. You are a fully Present, Conscious, living Being, awake and alert to the Presence of life in the moment. You are God, the life force energy within, manifested fully in the mind's right-standing position of wakefulness and Presence. Through this fully Present state of mind, there is exhibited power and intent; and this is the creative will of God, the will of life's unfolding of itself.

You have come to the shore of life, and all you need to do is get into the boat that has already been docked alongside the wharf. Its Presence has always been waiting for you. And as you set afloat in it, you will be guided along the river's natural flowing current, the natural path of life's unfolding. There is nothing to fear, as the river will guide you with its own power and strength, its own might. For it has already been set into motion. You are One with it now in your agreement of getting into the boat. You have agreed to align with it, One with life in the now of the reality of its existence.

We are all dreamers and visionaries through our creative imagination, an extension of the Creator, and in Him we desire to become and do more!

𝒜 PRESENT STATE OF MIND BRINGS YOU INTO A ONENESS AND AWARENESS OF LIFE; THE NATURAL FLOW OF GUIDANCE AND DIRECTION IS PRESENT, ENABLING YOU TO WALK OUT LIFE'S DESTINY.

For you formed my inward parts;
you knitted me together in my mother's womb.
I praise you, for I am fearfully and wonderfully made.
Wonderful are your works;
my soul knows it very well.
My frame was not hidden from you,
when I was being made in secret,
intricately woven in the depths of the earth.
Your eyes saw my unformed substance;
in your book were written, every one of them,
the days that were formed for me,
when as yet there was none of them.
(Psalm 139:13–16)

But when he who had set me apart before I was born, and who called me by his grace. (Galatians 1:15)

In him we have obtained an inheritance, having been predestined according to the purpose of him who works all things according to the counsel of his will .... (Ephesians 1:11)

For by him all things were created, in heaven and on earth, visible and invisible, whether thrones or dominions or rulers or authorities—all things were created through him and for him. (Colossians 1:16)

Everyone who is called by my name,
whom I created for my glory,
whom I formed and made. (Isaiah 43:7)

For I know the plans I have for you, declares the L<small>ORD</small>, **plans for welfare** and not for evil, **to give you a future and a hope.** *(Jeremiah 29:11)*

The L<small>ORD</small> of hosts has sworn:
"**As I have planned,**
    so shall it be,
and **as I have purposed,**
    so shall it stand ...." *(Isaiah 14:24)*

The L<small>ORD</small> has made everything for its purpose,
even the wicked for the day of trouble.
    (Proverbs 16:4)

Many are the **plans in the mind of a man,**
    but it is **the purpose of the L<small>ORD</small> that will stand.**
    (Proverbs 19:21)

The L<small>ORD</small> will fulfill his purpose for me;
    your steadfast love, O L<small>ORD</small>, **endures forever.**
    Do not forsake the work of your hands.
    (Psalm 138:8)

Declaring the end from the beginning
    and from ancient times things not yet done,
saying, "**My counsel shall stand,**
    and I will accomplish all my purpose ...."
    (Isaiah 46:10)

For it is God who works in you, both to will and to work for his good pleasure. *(Philippians 2:13)*

𝒟ISCOVERING LIFE'S INTENDED PURPOSE FOR YOU THROUGH A PRESENT STATE OF MIND.

Do not be conformed to this world, but be **transformed by the renewal of your mind,** *that by testing you* **may discern what is the will of God,** *what is good and acceptable and perfect. (Romans 12:2)*

> **The purpose in a man's heart is like deep water,**
> but **a man of understanding will draw it out.**
> *(Proverbs 20:5)*

But for this purpose I have raised you up, *to* **show you my power,** *so that my name may be proclaimed in all the earth. (Exodus 9:16)*

> **But they do not know**
> **the thoughts of the Lord;**
> **they do not understand his plan,**
> *that he has gathered them as sheaves to the*
> *threshing floor. (Micah 4:12)*

Not everyone who says to Me, "Lord, Lord," **will enter the kingdom of heaven, but he who does the will of My Father who is in heaven will enter.** *(Matthew 7:21)*

And he said, "The **God** *of our fathers* **appointed you to know his will,** *to* **see the Righteous One** *and* **to hear a voice from his mouth** ...." *(Acts 22:14)*

I can do nothing on my own. *As I hear, I judge, and my judgment is just, because* **I seek not my own** *will* **but the will of him who sent me.** *(John 5:30)*

Only **let each person lead the life that the Lord has assigned to him,** *and* **to which God has called him.** *This is my rule in all the churches. (1 Corinthians 7:17)*

⁊HE DRAWING IN OR CALLING OF GOD: LIFE'S PRESENCE IS DRAWING YOUR AWARENESS TO ITS REALITY. YOU ARE AWAKENING (ENLIGHTENED) TO LIFE IN THE NOW, THROUGH A PRESENT STATE OF MIND.

*I pray that **the eyes of your heart may be enlightened**, so that you will know what is the hope of His calling, what are the riches of the glory of His inheritance in the saints .... (Ephesians 1:18)*

*For the gifts and **the calling of God** are **irrevocable**. (Romans 11:29)*

*And we know that for those who love God all things work together for good, **for those who are called according to his purpose**. (Romans 8:28)*

⁊HE CONSCIOUS PRESENCE OF GOD WILL PLACE A BURNING DESIRE WITHIN YOU TO FULFULL THE PURPOSE FOR WHICH YOU HAVE BEEN CALLED (MADE AWARE OF).

*They said to each other, "**Did not our hearts burn within us while he talked to us** on the road, while he opened to us the Scriptures?" (Luke 24:32)*

Their leader will be one of their own;
*   **their ruler will arise** from among them.*
*   **I will bring him near and he will come close to me—***
*   **for who is he who will devote himself to be close to me?**'*
*   declares the LORD. (Jeremiah 30:21 NIV)*

Delight yourself in the LORD,
*   and **he will give you the desires of your heart**.*

Commit your way to the L<small>ORD</small>;
> trust in him, and he will act. *(Psalm 37:4–5)*

May he grant you your heart's desire
> **and fulfill all your plans**! *(Psalm 20:4)*

How blessed is **the one whom You choose and**
> **bring near to You**
> **To dwell** in Your courts
We will be satisfied with the goodness of Your house,
> Your holy temple. *(Psalm 65:4)*

I am my beloved's,
> **and his desire is for me.** *(Song of Solomon 7:10)*

$\mathcal{L}$ISTEN INTUITIVELY TO DIVINE DIRECTION THROUGH A PRESENT STATE OF MIND. THE PURPOSEFUL INTENT OF GOD WILL WORK THROUGH YOU WHEN YOU ARE THE LISTENING MIND, FULLY PRESENT TO WITNESS LIFE'S PATH.

O L<small>ORD</small>, the God of Abraham, Isaac, and Israel, our fathers, **keep forever such purposes** and **thoughts in the hearts of your people**, and **direct their hearts toward you**. *(1 Chronicles 29:18)*

And your ears shall hear a word behind you, saying, "**This is the way, walk in it**," when you turn to the right or when you turn to the left. *(Isaiah 30:21)*

> **I will instruct you and teach you in the way you**
> > **should go**;
> > **I will counsel you with my eye upon you**.
> > *(Psalm 32:8)*

> **Your word is a lamp to my feet**
> > and **a light to my path**. *(Psalm 119:105)*

> *The steps of a man are established by the* Lord,
> *when he delights in his way* …. *(Psalm 37:23)*

*For we are his workmanship, created in Christ Jesus **for good works, which God prepared beforehand, that we should walk in them***. *(Ephesians 2:10)*

$\mathcal{A}$S CHRIST DEMONSTRATED THROUGH THE DEATH OF THE EGO OR FALSE-SELF WILL (CONQUERING), WE BECOME ONE WITH THE PRESENCE OF LIFE AS OUR MINDS HAVE STOPPED SEEKING AND SURRENDERED TO A MENTAL STATE OF BEING PRESENT TO THE NOW. WE HAVE SOUGHT THE THINGS ABOVE (RAISED) THE RATIONALIZING MIND TO A HIGHER STATE OF CONCSCIOUS AWARENESS. THIS HIGHER STATE OF MIND IS FOUND IN THE RIGHT HEMISPHERE OF THE BRAIN (RIGHT HAND OF GOD), THE INTUITIVE AND CREATIVE STATE IN WHICH WE HAVE RISEN TO ACCESS THE KINGDOM OF GOD, THE DIVINE CREATOR.

Put On the New Self

If then you have been raised with Christ, seek the things that are above, where Christ is, seated at the right hand of God. (Colossians 3:1)

The one who conquers, I will grant him to sit with me on my throne, as I also conquered and sat down with my Father on his throne. (Revelation 3:21)

Chapter 5

The Book of Life—Remaining in the Eternal Presence of Life's Existence

Chapter 5.1

Fulfilling Your Destiny

Remain in the Metaphorical *Tree of Life* Found in the Metaphorical *Garden,* the Mind: Remain in a Present State of Mind to Fulfill Life's Destiny

You once were in darkness: the unconscious mind, the mind that is not aware of this Present moment, the mind that has fallen from Being Present to the reality of life's here and now existence. Your mind has now surrendered the false self-awareness and the ego identity that was created within the illusion outside of life's Presence. The mind is no longer caught up in its rationalizing, nor is it any longer seeking something which lies beyond life's existence, the here and now of reality. Your mind has now become still; it has transformed into the listening, witnessing, and observing mind, alert to life's Presence.

You have been transformed in the renewing of your mind through its awareness of witnessing life's occurring in the here and now. You have stepped out of the darkness, your unawareness of life's reality, and into the light of awareness of life's Presence. Your mind is fully alert, awake, and perceiving all that is. You are the observer to life, and in your awareness of it, you become One with it. Your mind is in its right position, fully aligned to the Conscious awareness of life's existence. You have been crowned with the gift of life, its true reality, this Present moment of your awareness to it. You have now reentered into the *Kingdom of God*, the existence of life's Presence, and you are positioned or seated on high having attained the highest functioning part of your brain, the creative intuitive Being. Through your Conscious awareness of Being One with life's occurring, your mind is open to the natural flow of wisdom and understanding of what is. Life's predetermined path has already been set out in its natural unfolding of itself. Now that you have come into an agreement or alignment with it, you are aware of your predestined purpose, and life's destiny is being fulfilled through you.

Continue to remain in the reality of life's Presence, this Present moment, to be intuitive to life's direction and guidance. Through your Conscious awareness of life's unfolding, you will naturally fulfill your purpose through life's infallible plan. You may fall out of Presence again through the mind's being led astray by its false self-awareness or by beginning to reflect on the past or the future, which are illusions to the reality of life's Presence. When this occurs, ground your mind to an awareness of your Present surroundings, coming back to Conscious awareness to life's reality. Continue to overcome the mind that continues to separate itself from life's Presence by surrendering to the here and now. It is a continual process of renewing your mind's position to remain in life's existence.

The more you remain in *the Tree of Life,* continuing to be Present with life's reality, you become aware of life's purpose and plan; and the more your mind exists in the Present moment of awareness of life, you are One with the manifestation of your destiny.

Allow life's unfolding to reveal its purpose and plan for your existence. You are the extension of Infinite Intelligence, fully in alignment with the life force energy that is within and all around you! You have access to life's wisdom, knowledge, understanding, guidance, and direction. You are One with the unlimited Infinite Source of all life existence. Continue to be Present of mind at all times, Consciously aware, having an alert mind, and listening intuitively.

𝒥ALLING AWAY FROM ME

Is your focus upon Me, My Presence of life's only reality? Have you revered life in this moment of its existence? Where does your mind wander, child? Has it led you astray from what is? Surely you are unaware that you have fallen away from Me, the existence of life! The world and its enticements have lured your mind away from Me. I cannot be found in the world. I am inward, within you, through your Conscious awareness of life: that is Me! I have never left you! Indeed, I AM always Present. For I AM the existence of life's Presence within and all around you. Come back to our meeting place, this Present moment of life. Come dwell in the heavenly realm, the Eternal life Presence. Come sit, and be comforted in your awareness of My existence. I AM your Being and aliveness, the Creator of your existence; I AM the life force energy that is sustaining you in this Present moment of time. Shall you not, for just a moment, take your eyes off the world's distractions and seeking for more, and enter My Presence of life's existence? The reality of life awaits you! Come, remain in Me, for your destiny awaits you.

Remain in Me, life in this moment, as I, your life force energy, remains in you. Together as One, we will accomplish all I have set out for you.

Remain in the vine, the branch of life. Be awakened to the unfolding of life's Presence in the here and now!

The more you are in My Presence, the less you desire of the world. The more you remain in the Present, the things of the world fall away from you.

Your journey begins in following Me out of this world's illusion and into the reality of the existence of life. The here and now, Present of time.

"In the beginning was the Word, and the Word was with God, and the Word was God ...."

The Book of Life Has an Author and Perfector

God, *the Word*, is the author of the book called Life; that is what He first imagined and envisioned the world to be. The Words of the book were revealed through inspiration given to His scribes who would write the scriptures, later forming the author's manuscript.

The manuscript of *the Book of Life* foretells the great mystery of life's existence and its unfolding plan for all.

Through life's great vision, the creation or play of life was spoken into existence. The world is the stage for the performance called life and you have a role in it. There is one catch, however: your purpose is hidden deep within you and can only be brought to the light of your awareness through your Consciousness. You must seek out your true identity by aligning your mind with the Presence or reality of life to know your role, and your purpose in the play called life.

God is the director of this play called life. You have been handed a role in the performance, which is your purpose; allow the Director to guide you in your delivery of your role. Sign up with the Director to receive your role and remain in the unfolding of the play! For in *The Book of Life*, the script has already been written, and the purposes have already been allotted. All has been accounted for.

$\mathcal{I}$N THE BEGINNING OF CREATION WAS THE WORD (GOD). ALL THINGS MADE BY GOD WERE SPOKEN INTO EXISTENCE HAVING THE AWARENESS (LIGHT) OF LIFE IN THEM.

In the beginning was the Word, and the Word was with God, and the Word was God.

The same was in the beginning with God.

All things were made by him; and without him was not any thing made that was made.

In him was life; and the life was the light of men. (John 1:1-4 KJV)

$\mathcal{T}$HE BOOK OF LIFE: THE REALITY OF YOUR LIFE'S PREDESTINED EXISTENCE.

And we know that in all things God works for the good of those who love him, who have been called according to his purpose. For those God foreknew he also predestined to be conformed to the image of his Son, that he might be the firstborn among many brothers and sisters. And those he predestined, he also called; those he called, he also justified; those he justified, he also glorified. (Romans 8:28-30)

> *Your eyes saw my unformed substance;*
> *in your book were written, every one of them,*
> > *the days that were formed for me,*
> > *when as yet there was none of them. (Psalm 139:16)*

$\mathcal{A}$LIGN YOUR MIND'S POSTION TO A PRESENT STATE OF AWARENESS TO REMAIN IN LIFE'S BOOK (PREDESTINY).

*So Moses returned to the L*ORD *and said, "Alas, this people has sinned* **a great sin***. They have made for themselves gods of gold. But now, if you will forgive their sin—but if not,* **please blot me out of your book that you have written***." But the L*ORD *said to Moses, "***Whoever has sinned against me, I will blot out of my book***." (Exodus 32:31–33)*

Then I saw a great white throne and him who was seated on it. From his presence earth and sky fled away, and no place was found for them. And I saw the dead, great and small, standing before the throne, and **books were opened***. Then another book was opened, which is* **the book of life***. And the dead were judged by what was written in the books, according to what they had done. (Revelation 20:11–12)*

This is the second death, the lake of fire. And if **anyone's name was not found written in the book of life***, he was thrown into the lake of fire. (Revelation 20:14–15)*

And all who dwell on earth will worship it, everyone **whose name has not been written before the foundation of the world in the book of life** *of the Lamb who was slain. (Revelation 13:8)*

$\mathcal{A}$ MIND THAT IS NOT IN A RIGHT STANDING POSITION OF BEING PRESENT OR AWARE OF LIFE'S REALITY.

Let them be blotted out of the book of the living;
   let them not be enrolled among the **righteous***.*
   (Psalm 69:28)

$\mathcal{C}$ ONQUERING THE FALSE SELF-AWARENESS TO GAIN A PRESENT STATE OF MIND THAT IS AWARE (WHITE GARMENTS REFLECTING THE LIGHT OR AWARENESS OF LIFE) OF LIFE IN THE NOW.

The one who conquers will be clothed thus in **white garments, and I will never blot his name out of the book of life**. I will confess his name before my Father and before his angels. *(Revelation 3:5)*

ℒO EAT OF THE TREE OF LIFE IS TO BE PRESENT TO ITS REALITY; THE PARADISE OF GOD IS A PRESENT STATE OF MIND (RIGHTEOUSNESS).

He who has an ear, let him hear what the Spirit says to the churches. **To the one who conquers I will grant to eat of the tree of life**, which is in **the paradise of God**. *(Revelation 2:7)*

The fruit of the righteous is *a tree of life*, and whoever captures souls is wise. *(Proverbs 11:30)*

𝒴OU HAVE ENTERED A PRESENT STATE OF MIND (HEAVEN; THE PARADISE OF GOD) AND ARE NOW EATING FROM THE FRUIT (KNOWLEDGE OF ITS REALITY) OF THE TREE OF LIFE.

Nevertheless, do not rejoice in this, that the spirits are subject to you, but **rejoice that your names are written in heaven**. *(Luke 10:20)*

𝒥F THE MIND STRAYS FROM PRESENCE THE GOOD NEWS (GOSPEL) IS THAT YOU CAN BRING YOUR MIND'S AWARENESS BACK (REPENT) TO THE PRESENCE OF LIFE'S REALITY: COME BACK TO A PRESENT STATE OF MIND.

Then the LORD God said, "Behold, the man has become like one of us in knowing good and evil. **Now, lest he reach out his hand and take also of the tree of life and eat, and live forever**...." *(Genesis 3:22)*

*From that time Jesus began to preach, saying, "**Repent, for the kingdom of heaven is at hand.**" (Matthew 4:17)*

ℛEMAINING IN THE TREE OF LIFE IS THE MIND THAT REMAINS PRESENT (ABIDE IN ME) TO THE AWARENESS OF LIFE (AND I IN YOU) IN THE NOW. REMAINING PRESENT ALLOWS THE MANIFESTATION OF GOD, THE LIFE FORCE ENERGY, THE DIVINE CREATOR TO FLOW THROUGH YOU.

I Am the True Vine

*"**I am the true vine, and my Father is the vinedresser. Every branch in me that does not bear fruit he takes away, and every branch that does bear fruit he prunes, that it may bear more fruit.** Already you are clean because of the word that I have spoken to you. **Abide in me, and I in you.** As **the branch cannot bear fruit by itself, unless it abides in the vine**, neither can you, unless you abide in me. I am the vine; you are the branches. **Whoever abides in me and I in him, he it is that bears much fruit, for apart from me you can do nothing.** (John 15:1-5)*

𝒲HEN YOU ARE PRESENT OF MIND (LAY HOLD) TO LIFE'S REALITY REMAIN PRESENT (HOLD FAST) TO ITS EXISTENCE.

***She is a tree of life to those who lay hold of her;** **those who hold her fast** are called blessed.* *(Proverbs 3:18)*

Chapter 5.2

Your Mission—Life's Last Instruction

You Now Have the Witnessing Testimony to Your Observation of Life's Present Reality!

It is you, oh sleeper, who has awakened to the light of My Presence. And you see Me as I AM, life in this Present moment. For you have awakened in your awareness of life's only existence, this Present time, this time now at hand! Come and eat the fruit of life that My Father has prepared before the foundation of the earth ….

Once you are awakened in the light of your awareness of the Presence of Life, found only in the Present Moment, see to it that you too deliver the good news to all ….

*T*HE GREATEST REVELATION AND MYSTERY MADE KNOWN: THE KINGDOM OF GOD IS A PRESENT STATE OF MIND. THE EXISTENCE OF LIFE'S PRESENCE IS FOUND IN THE HERE AND NOW OF REALITY.

*But **you will receive power when the Holy Spirit comes on you**; and **you will be** my **witnesses** in Jerusalem, and in all Judea and Samaria, and to the ends of the earth. (Acts 1:8)*

*S*HARE YOUR TESTIMONY (SPEAK THE TRUTH) OF YOUR AWARENESS (WHAT WE HAVE SEEN) OF THE INTERNAL CONSCIOUS VOICE (WISDOM AND UNDERSTANDING) OF GOD THAT IS IN ALL AND THROUGH ALL.

For we cannot but speak of what we have seen and heard. (Acts 4:20)

Appendices

Appendix 1

A Practice of Enlightenment: Entering into the Light of Awareness—A Present State of Mind

Seek a place of little distraction, a secluded place away from the world, free from any interference that may cause the mind to stray and not focus. Enter into a state of mind that is free of thought by surrendering each thought that arises within your mind. This is the process of freeing the mind and your attachment with it. Ten minutes or so of music may help bring the mind to this higher state of awareness because the mind is listening rather than continually thinking or rationalizing. The sights and sounds of nature, such as rushing waters, may also help to bring the mind to an observing or listening state. In the book of Revelation, John describes Jesus's voice as the sound of rushing water. His voice is also described as loud thunder or mighty ocean waves. I always find that during a period of singing or listening to music, my thoughts become free in those experiences because my mind has transitioned to a stance of listening. My mind's state has transformed from the rationalizing and thinking mind to the listening intuitive mind. I am fully Present of mind, having my mind's position aligned with the listening or observing state of awareness. You want to come to a position within your mind in which you are no longer thinking but waiting in silence, as if waiting to hear. Be patient, and continue to wait for the mind to transition into the higher state of Being through awareness where the intuitive and creative energy emerges.

It may help to have a pen and paper nearby so as to wait for the inspired word to come to you. In your waiting, you are the observing mind, the witnessing mind, which is fully alert, awake, and ready to hear. Your mind is not set on the past or the future but fully positioned in the here and now, this Present moment. Your mind's renewal to a stillness, coming into an awareness of what is now occurring, is your enlightenment. You have stepped out of the dark, your mind's unawareness to life's Present occurring, and have entered into the light of awareness, life's Present reality in this moment.

You have been crowned with life in your awareness to its now occurring. Your mind is still, having come to an awareness; it is observing and witnessing life as it is. This is your moment of salvation, the end of your mind's suffering of being in the dark or the mind's unawareness to life.

Remember, God, the life force energy within you is *the Word*. Wait with a listening mind, and the inspired *Word*, the voice of God, will arise within your Consciousness ....

> **Make a joyful noise to the LORD,** *all the earth!*
>> **Serve the LORD with gladness!**
>> **Come into his presence with singing!**
> *Know that the LORD, he is God!*
>> *It is he who made us, and we are his;*
>> *we are his people, and the sheep of his pasture.*
> **Enter his gates with thanksgiving,**
>> *and* **his courts with praise!**
>> **Give thanks to him; bless his name!**
> *(Psalm 100:1–4)*

A Prayer Seeking God's Voice

My Lord, I will continue to seek your Presence within my mind. I will quiet my self, surrendering the thoughts that lead my mind astray from Being Present with You in this moment. I will call upon Your name and wait for Your Presence to emerge within my awareness. Come to me, dear Lord. As I wait here in the silence of my mind, reveal Yourself to me. I will be still now, for You are God! Enter my Conscious awareness, and manifest within my mind and my thoughts! Speak Your thoughts to me, Lord! I will wait and listen, in the stillness of my mind, for You to enter ….

But when you pray, go into your room and shut the door and **pray to your Father who is in secret**. **And your Father who sees in secret will reward you.**

And when you pray, do not heap up empty phrases as the Gentiles do, **for they think that they will be heard for their many words**. *(Matthew 6:6–7)*

Appendix 2

Bibliography

1. www.openbible.info (English Standard Version)
2. www.biblegateway.com/ (English Standard Version)
3. www.intouch.org
4. www.merriam-webster.com
5. www.wikipedia.org
6. plato.stanford.edu/entries/pineal-gland/ Descartes and the Pineal Gland
7. biblehub.com
8. thejubileebible.com
9. www.biblica.com/resources/bible-faqs/ in-what-language-was-the-bible-first-written
10. www.biblegateway.com/blog/2012/06/ what-was-the-original-language-of-the-bible

About the Author

Tracy Menchenton with more than twenty years experience in law enforcement felt internally driven at a young age to explore and investigate the darkened mind of the unconscious experience. As she recounts in this eloquent case for seeking the Presence of God, her personal journey unfolds to the supernatural awakenings of the voice of God within. Losing all identity of who *she thought to be*, having suffered through many personal trials of her life, she surrendered her false self awareness and sought to find God in the midst of her pain. For purely altruistic reasons through the Divine calling and greater purpose, she was guided along in Spirit to write the wisdom of this book.

Tracy Menchenton lives in Calgary Alberta with her young and vibrant daughter, and their rescued dog, Rosa. She is currently writing a sequel to *My Thoughts Become Your Thoughts*.